EASY PIANO

TOP HITS OF 2022

SEVENTEEN OF THE YEAR'S BEST SONGS

ISBN 978-1-70517-632-0

HAL•LEONARD®

Visit Hal Leonard Online at
www.halleonard.com

World headquarters, contact:
Hal Leonard
7777 West Bluemound Road
Milwaukee, WI 53213
Email: info@halleonard.com

In Europe, contact:
Hal Leonard Europe Limited
1 Red Place
London, W1K 6PL
Email: info@halleonardeurope.com

In Australia, contact:
Hal Leonard Australia Pty. Ltd.
4 Lentara Court
Cheltenham, Victoria, 3192 Australia
Email: info@halleonard.com.au

10 **AS IT WAS**
HARRY STYLES

3 **BAM BAM**
CAMILA CABELLO FT. ED SHEERAN

16 **BOTH SIDES NOW**
EMILIA CLARKE (featured in CODA)

26 **CAROLINA**
TAYLOR SWIFT (from WHERE THE CRAWDADS SING)

32 **ENEMY**
IMAGINE DRAGONS

38 **FREEDOM**
JON BATISTE

46 **GLIMPSE OF US**
JOJI

50 **HOLD MY HAND**
LADY GAGA (from TOP GUN: MAVERICK)

19 **IN THE STARS**
BENSON BOONE

60 **LIGHT SWITCH**
CHARLIE PUTH

55 **LOVE ME MORE**
SAM SMITH

66 **NOBODY LIKE U**
from TURNING RED

72 **NUMB LITTLE BUG**
EM BEIHOLD

78 **ON MY WAY**
JENNIFER LOPEZ (from MARRY ME)

84 **RUNNING UP THAT HILL**
KATE BUSH (featured in STRANGER THINGS)

92 **'TIL YOU CAN'T**
CODY JOHNSON

100 **UNTIL I FOUND YOU**
STEPHEN SANCHEZ

BAM BAM

Words and Music by CAMILA CABELLO,
ED SHEERAN, SCOTT HARRIS,
ERIC FREDERIC, EDGAR BARRERA
and CHECHE ALARA

Syncopated Acoustic Pop

You said you hat-ed the o - cean, but you're surf-ing now.

I said I'd love you for life, __ but I just sold our house.

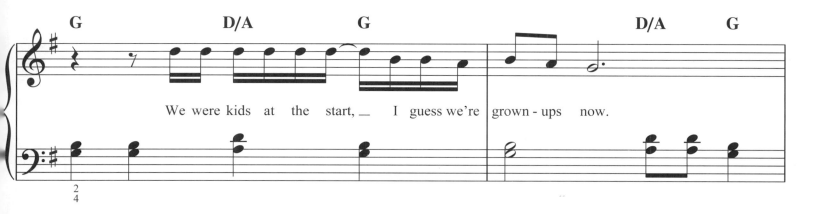

We were kids at the start, __ I guess we're grown - ups now.

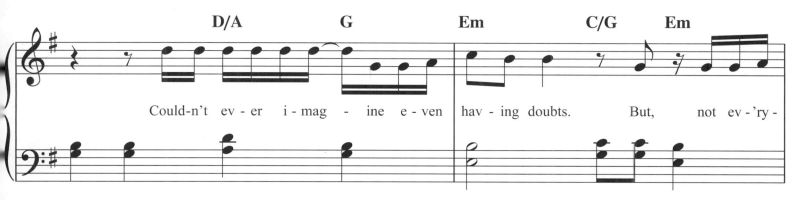

Could-n't ev - er i-mag - ine e - ven hav - ing doubts. But, not ev-'ry-

4

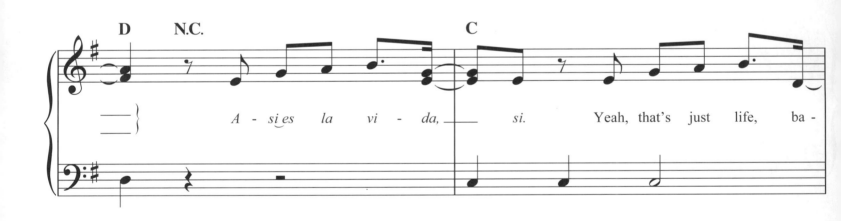

feet. A-si es la vi-da, ___ si. Yeah, that's just life, ba - by. I was bare-ly stand-

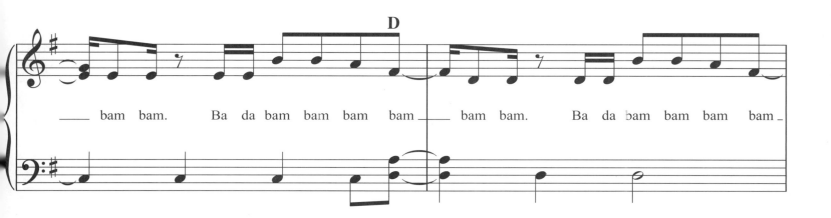

- ing, but now I'm danc - ing, he's all o - ver me. Ba da bam bam bam bam ___

___ bam bam. Ba da bam bam bam bam ___ bam bam. Ba da bam bam bam bam ___

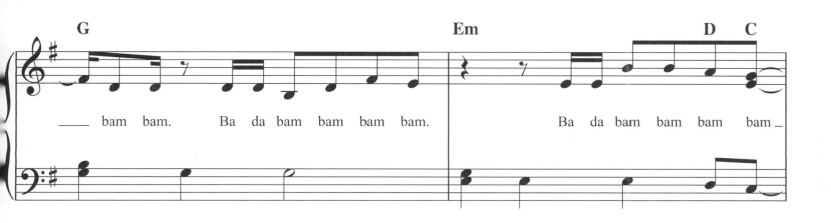

___ bam bam. Ba da bam bam bam bam. Ba da bam bam bam bam ___

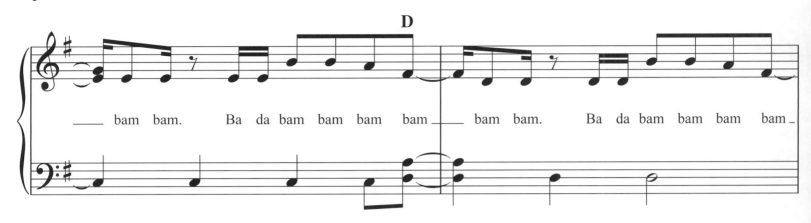

bam bam. Ba da bam bam bam bam ____ bam bam. Ba da bam bam bam bam ____

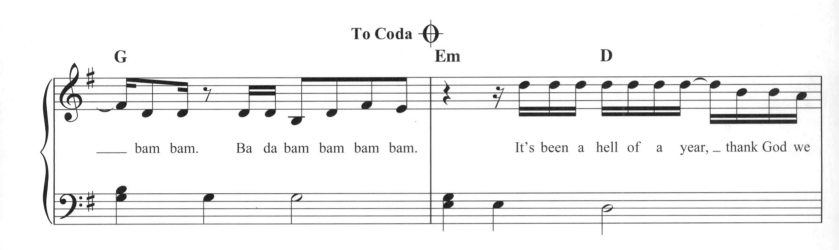

bam bam. Ba da bam bam bam bam. It's been a hell of a year, ___ thank God we

made it out. Yeah, we were rid-ing a wave ___ and try-ing

not to drown. And on the sur-face I held it to-geth-er but un-der-neath I sort-a

came a-round. Where would I be? You're all that I need. _ My world, ba-by, you

D.S. al Coda

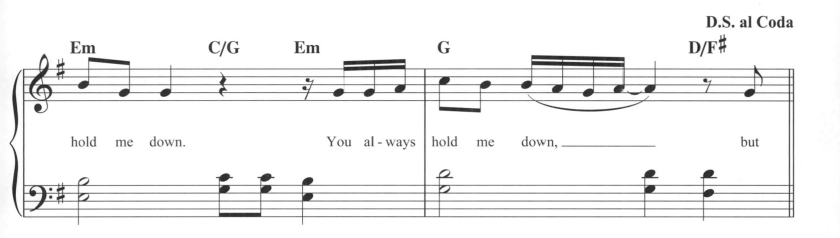

hold me down. You al-ways hold me down, _____ but

CODA

Pón-gan-le a-zu - car mi gen - te! *Y si-gue bai-lan - do.* _

_ *Y si-gue bai-lan - do.* _ *Y si-gue bai-lan - do.* _ *Y si-gue bai-lan - do.* _

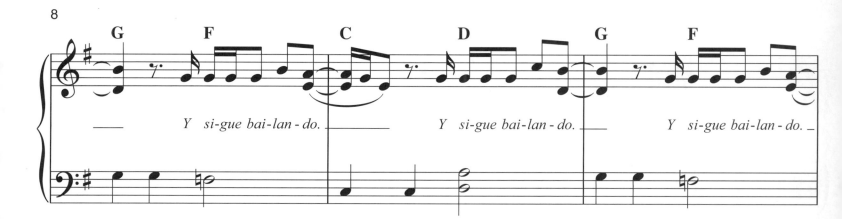

Y si-gue bai-lan-do. Y si-gue bai-lan-do. Y si-gue bai-lan-do.

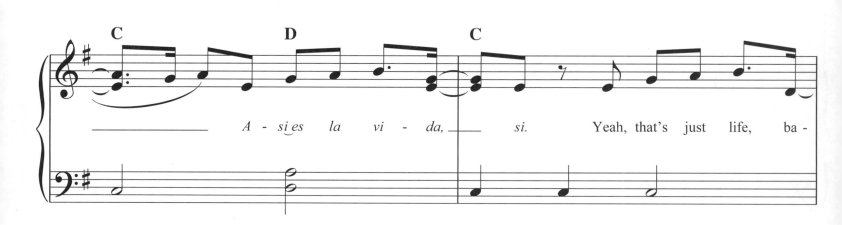

A - si es la vi - da, si. Yeah, that's just life, ba -

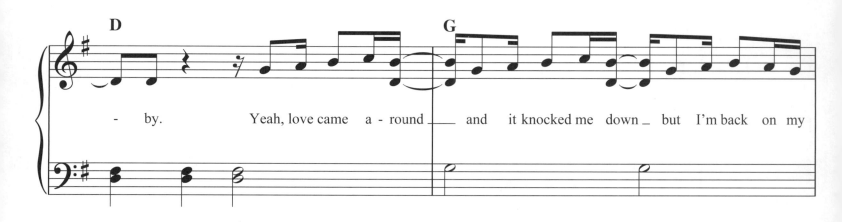

- by. Yeah, love came a - round and it knocked me down but I'm back on my

feet. A-si es la vi-da, si. Yeah, that's just life, ba - by. I was bare-ly stand-

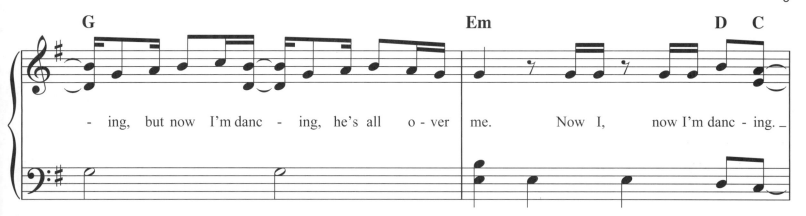

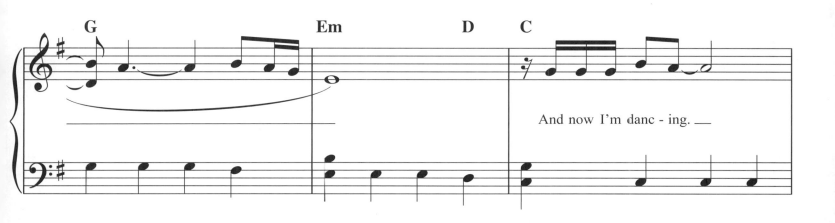

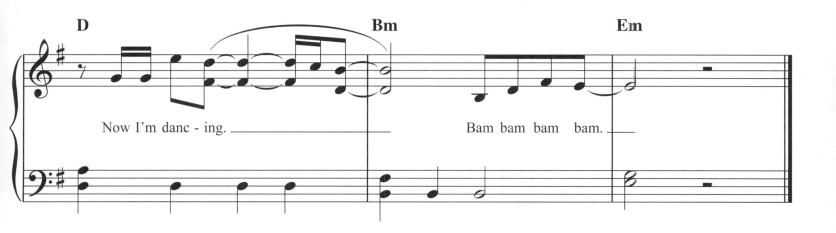

AS IT WAS

Words and Music by HARRY STYLES,
THOMAS HULL and TYLER JOHNSON

With energy

Hold- ing me back, ___
An - swer the phone, ___

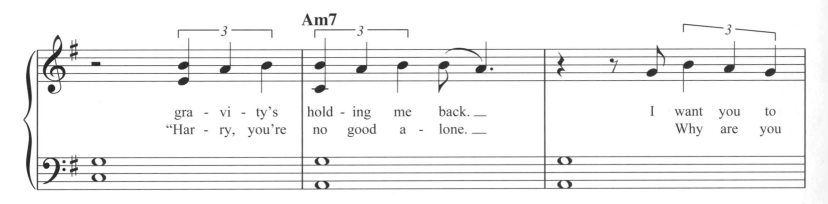

gra - vi - ty's hold- ing me back. ___   I want you to
"Har - ry, you're no good a - lone. ___   Why are you

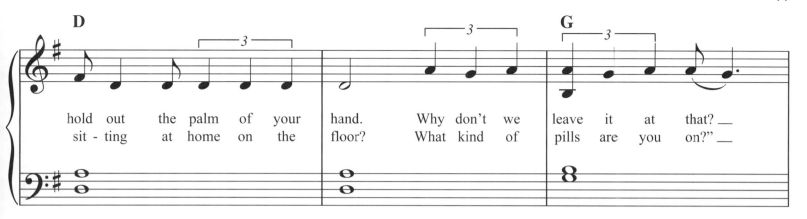

hold out the palm of your | hand. Why don't we | leave it at that? —
sit - ting at home on the | floor? What kind of | pills are you on?" —

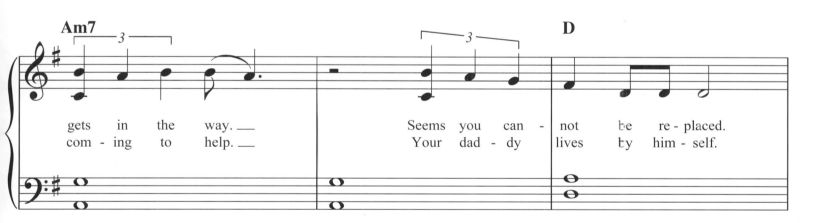

Noth - ing to say ___ | when ev - 'ry - thing
Ring - ing the bell ___ | and no - bod - y's

gets in the way. ___ | Seems you can - not be re - placed.
com - ing to help. ___ | Your dad - dy lives by him - self.

And I'm the | one who will stay. ___ | Oh. ___
He just wants to | know that you're well. ___ | Oh. ___

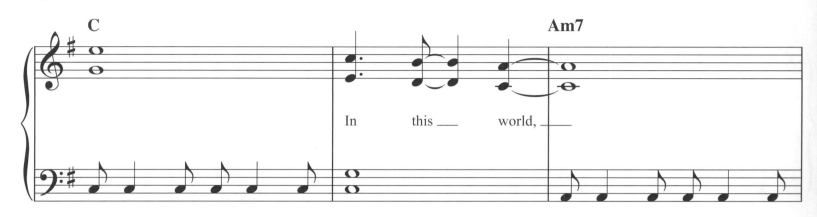

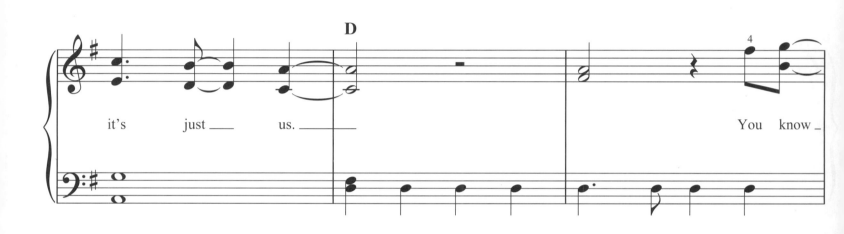

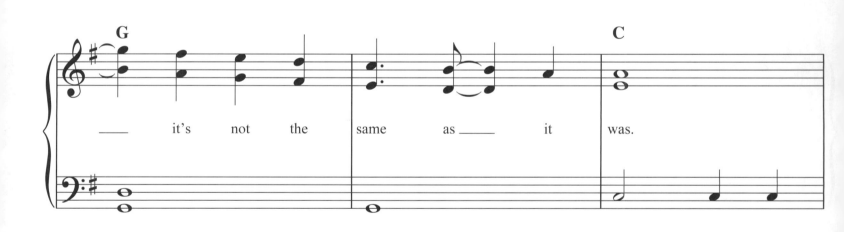

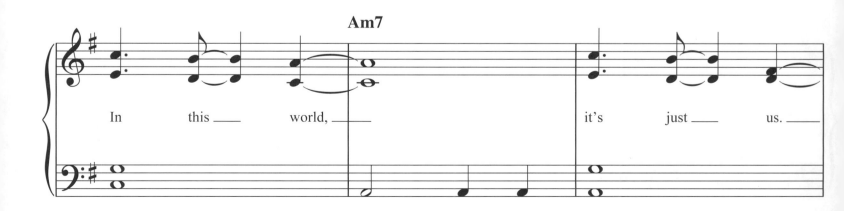

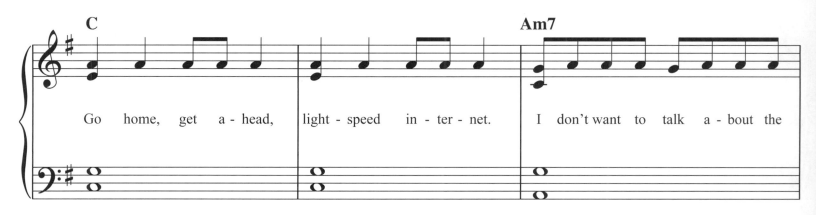

C   **Am7**

Go home, get a - head, light - speed in - ter - net. I don't want to talk a - bout the

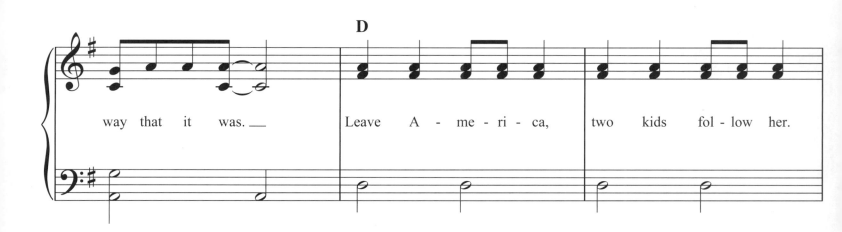

D

way that it was. ___ Leave A - me - ri - ca, two kids fol - low her.

G   **N.C.**

I don't want to talk a - bout who's do - ing it first. ___

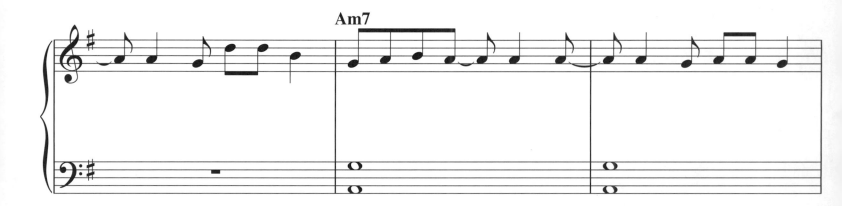

Am7

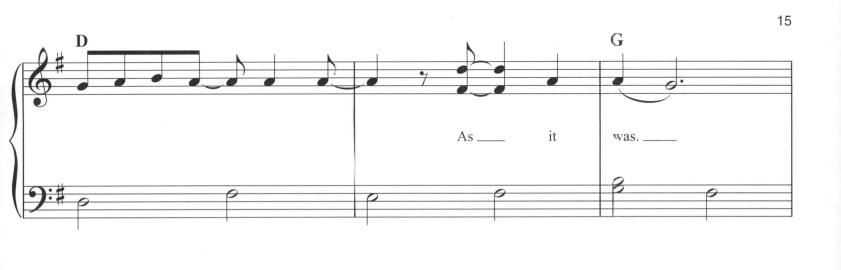

As ___ it was. ___

You know ___ it's not the same as ___ it was.

As ___ it was.

As ___ it was. ___

BOTH SIDES NOW

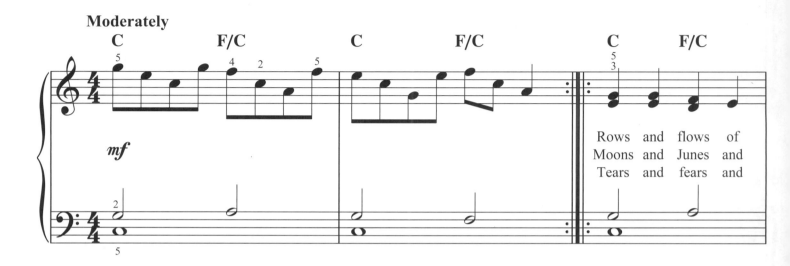

Words and Music by
JONI MITCHELL

Moderately

Rows and flows of
Moons and Junes and
Tears and fears and

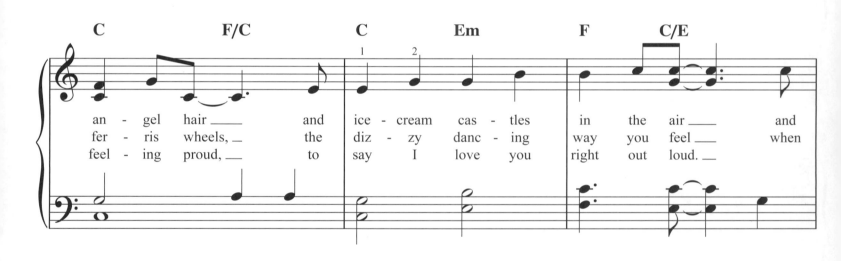

an - gel hair ____ and ice-cream cas - tles in the air ____ and
fer - ris wheels, __ the diz - zy danc - ing way you feel ____ when
feel - ing proud, __ to say I love you right out loud. ____

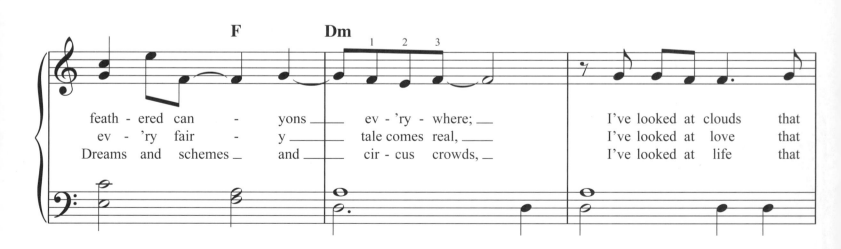

feath - ered can - yons ____ ev - 'ry - where; __ I've looked at clouds that
ev - 'ry fair - y tale comes real, ____ I've looked at love that
Dreams and schemes _ and cir - cus crowds, _ I've looked at life that

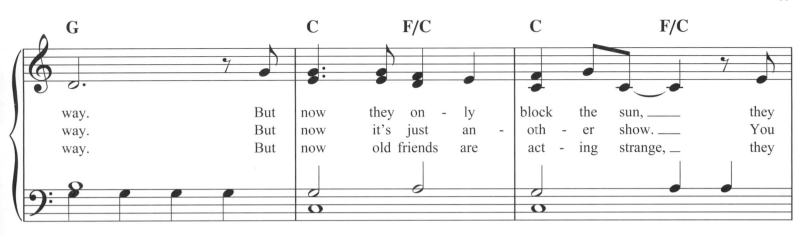

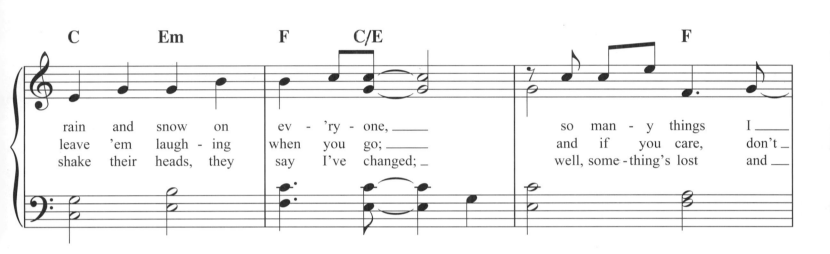

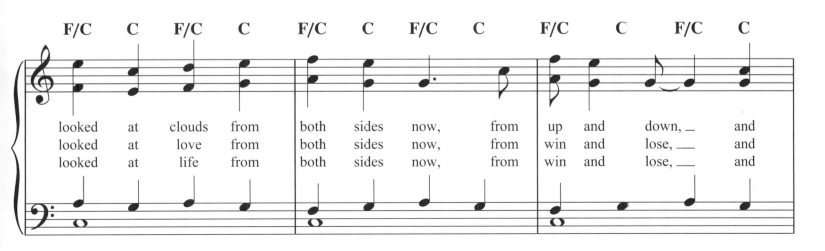

18

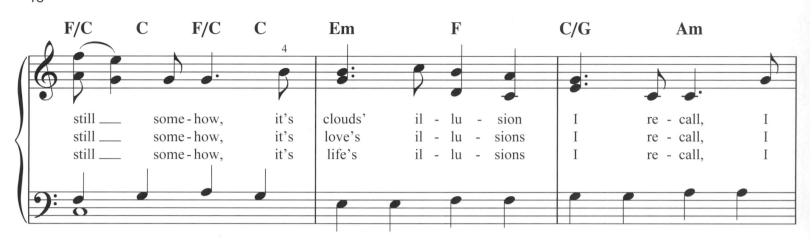

still ___ some-how, it's clouds' il - lu - sion I re - call, I
still ___ some-how, it's love's il - lu - sions I re - call, I
still ___ some-how, it's life's il - lu - sions I re - call, I

real - ly ___ don't know clouds ___ at ___
real - ly ___ don't know love ___ at ___
real - ly ___ don't know life ___ at ___

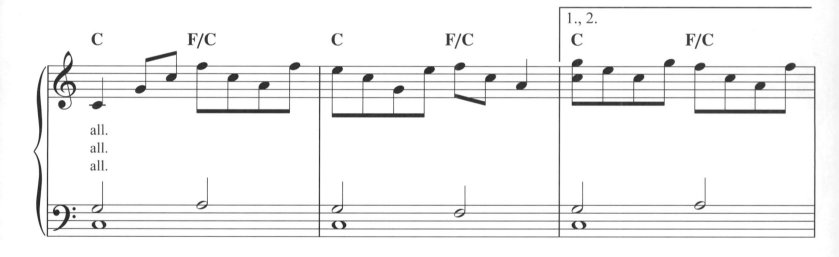

all.
all.
all.

rit.

IN THE STARS

Words and Music by BENSON BOONE,
MICHAEL POLLACK and JASON EVIGAN

Pop Ballad

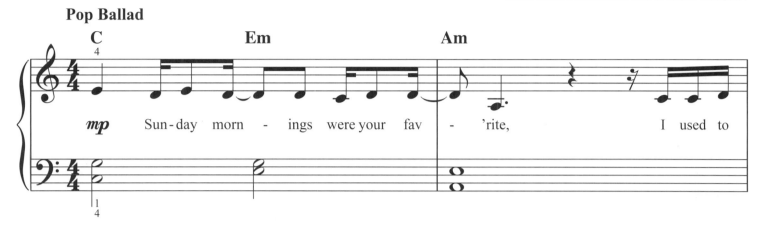

Sun-day morn-ings were your fav-'rite, I used to

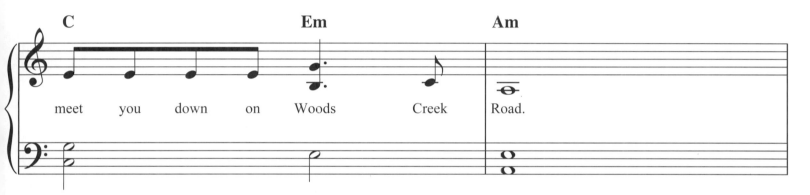

meet you down on Woods Creek Road.

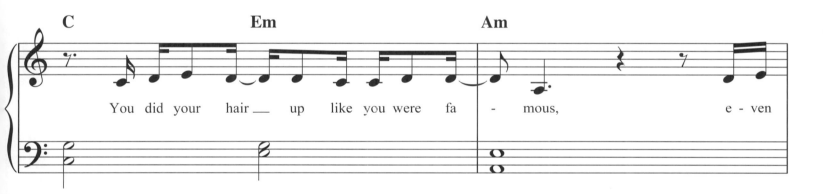

You did your hair up like you were fa-mous, e-ven

though it's on-ly church where we were go-ing. Now,

Sun - day morn - ings, I just sleep ___ in, it's like I've

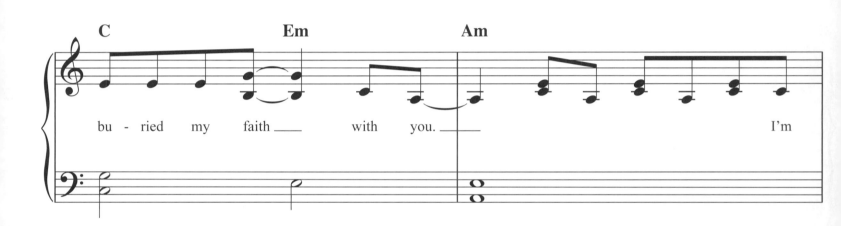

bu - ried my faith ___ with you. ___ I'm

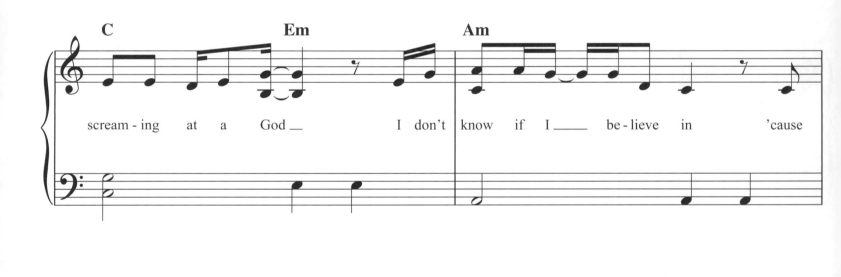

scream - ing at a God ___ I don't know if I ___ be - lieve in 'cause

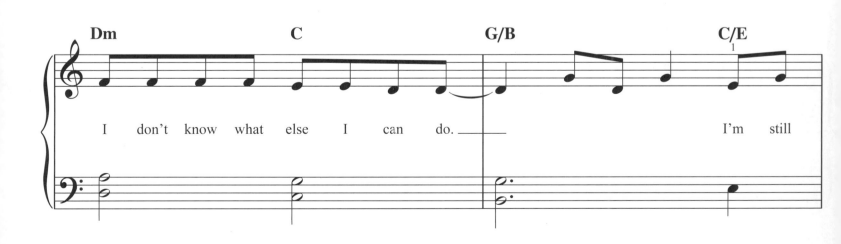

I don't know what else I can do. ___ I'm still

hold - ing on to ev - 'ry - thing that's dead and gone. I don't want to

say good-bye 'cause this one means for-ev - er. _____ Now you're

in the stars and six feet's nev - er felt so far. Here I am a-

lone be-tween the heav - ens and the em - bers. _____ Oh, _____ it

hurts so hard _____ for a mil - lion dif - f'rent rea - sons. You took the

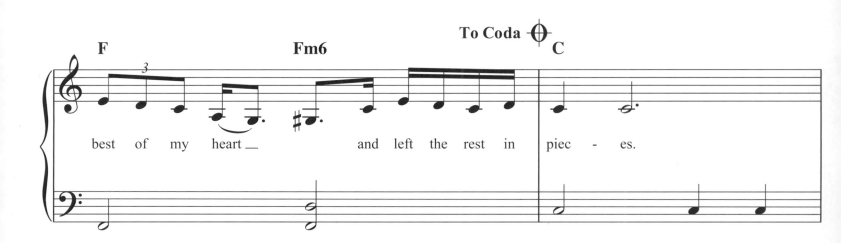

best of my heart __ and left the rest in piec - es.

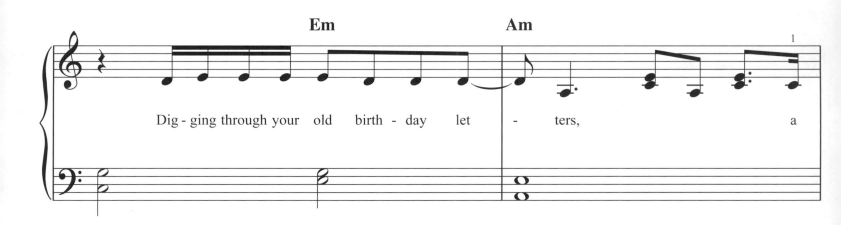

Dig - ging through your old birth - day let - ters, a

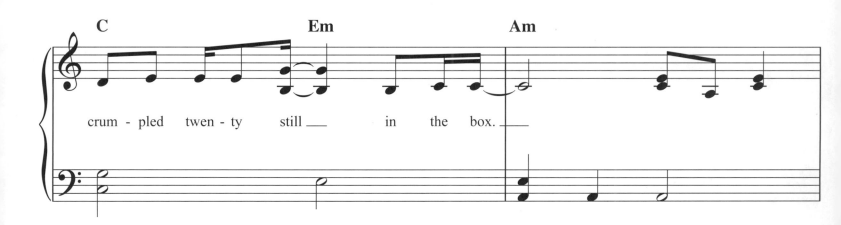

crum - pled twen - ty still __ in the box. __

I don't think that I ____ could ev - er find a way ____ to spend ____ it ev - en

D.S. al Coda

if it's the last twen - ty that I've got. Oh, I'm still

CODA

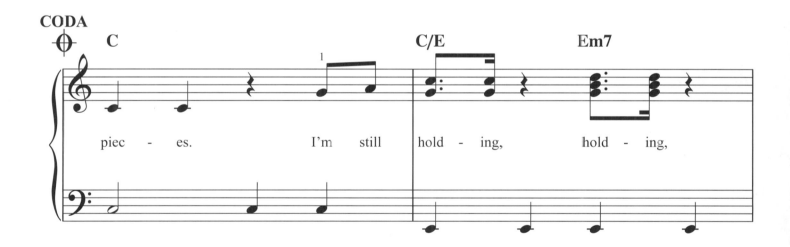

piec - es. I'm still hold - ing, hold - ing,

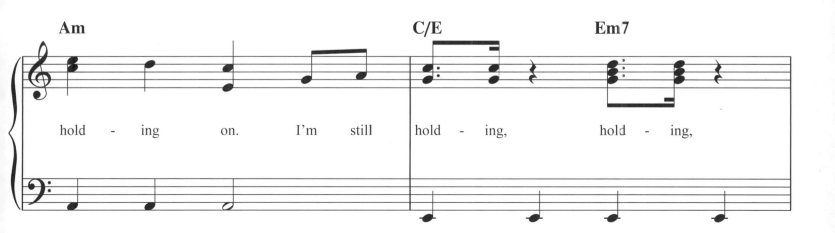

hold - ing on. I'm still hold - ing, hold - ing,

hold - ing on. I'm still hold - ing, hold - ing,

hold - ing on. I'm still ooh, still hold - ing on. I'm still

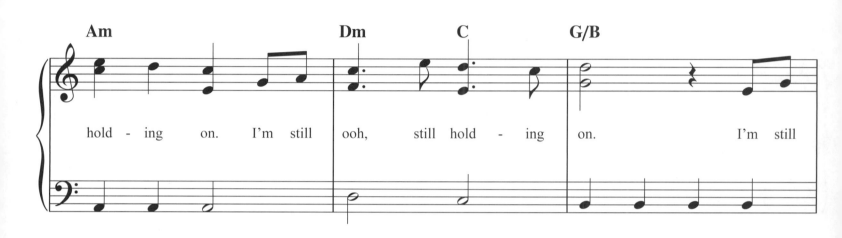

hold - ing on to ev - 'ry - thing that's dead and gone. I don't want to

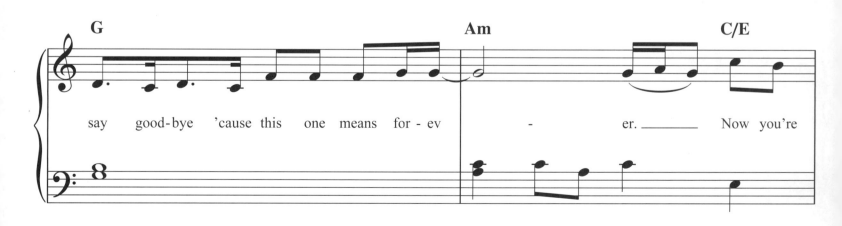

say good-bye 'cause this one means for - ev - er. _____ Now you're

in the stars and six feet's nev - er felt so far. Here I am a-

lone be - tween the heav - ens and __ the em - bers. __ Oh, _____ it

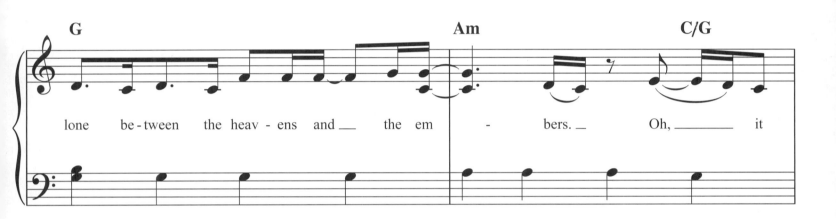

hurts so hard _____ for a mil - lion dif-f'rent rea - sons. You took the

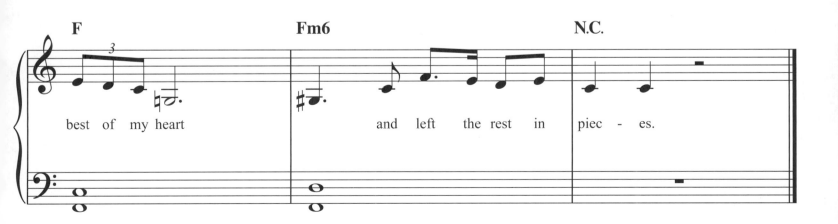

best of my heart and left the rest in piec - es.

CAROLINA
from WHERE THE CRAWDADS SING

Words and Music by
TAYLOR SWIFT

Moderately

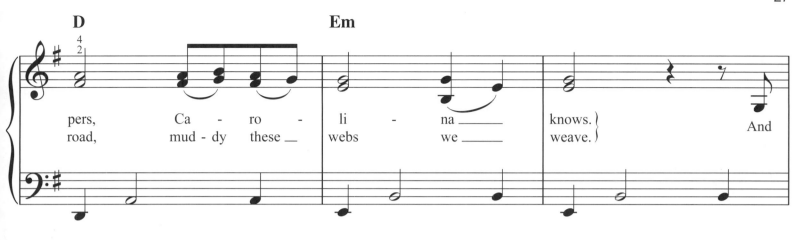

count. And there are plac - es I will nev-er ev-er go. ____

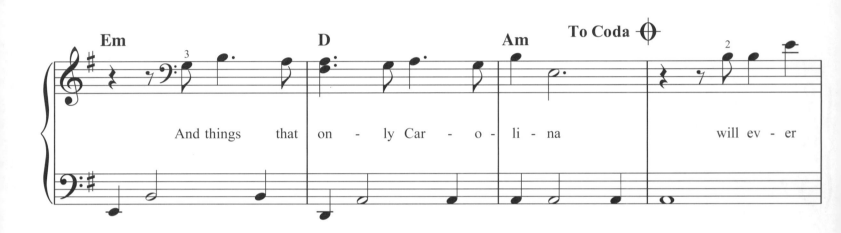

And things that on - ly Car - o - li - na will ev - er

To Coda ⊕

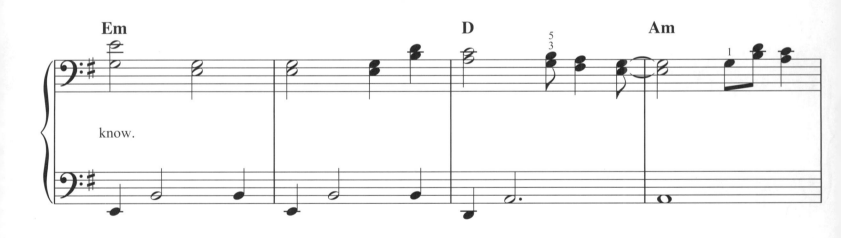

know.

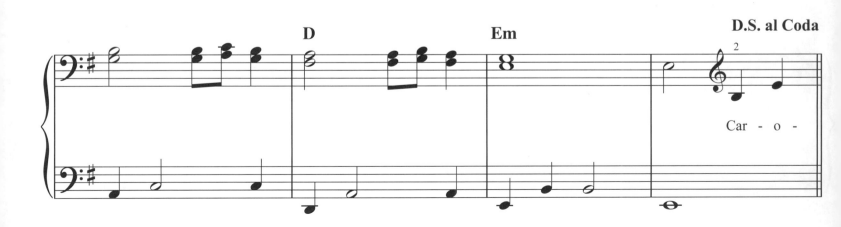

D.S. al Coda

Car - o -

CODA

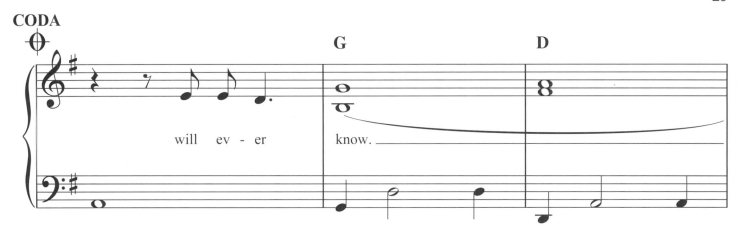

will ev - er know.

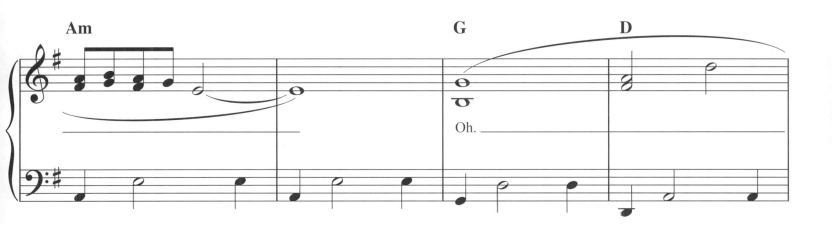

Oh.

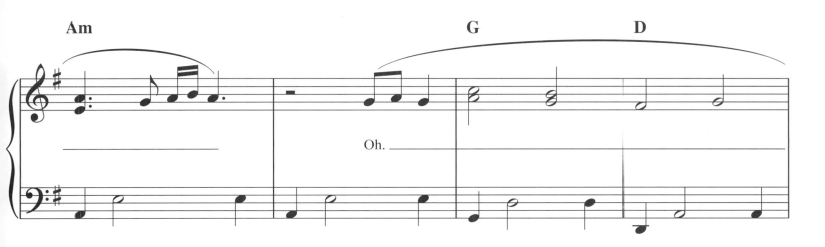

Oh.

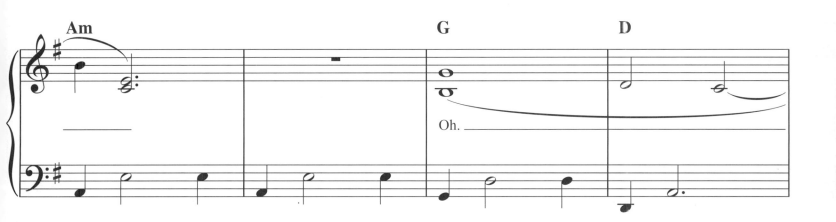

Oh.

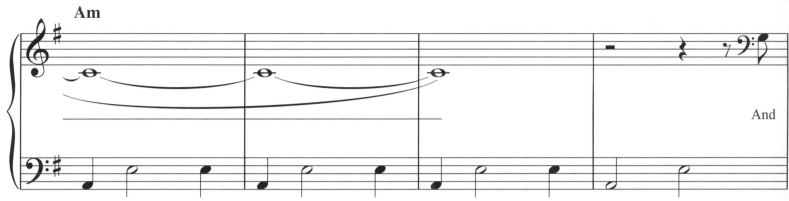

And

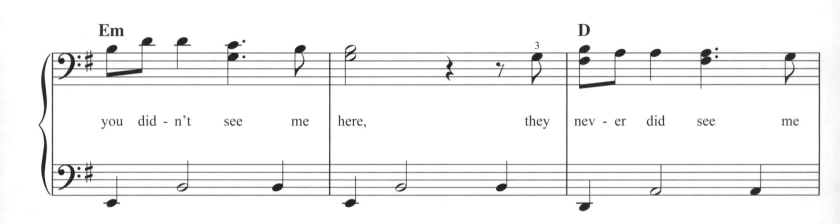

you did - n't see me here, they nev - er did see me

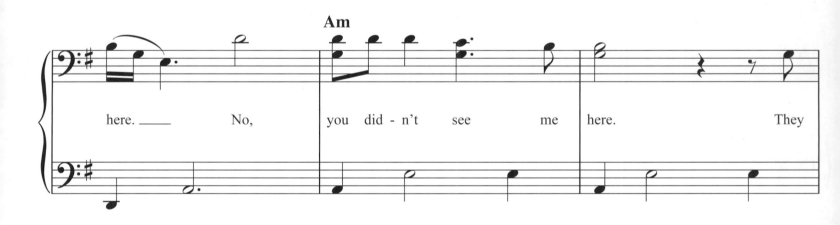

here. _____ No, you did - n't see me here. They

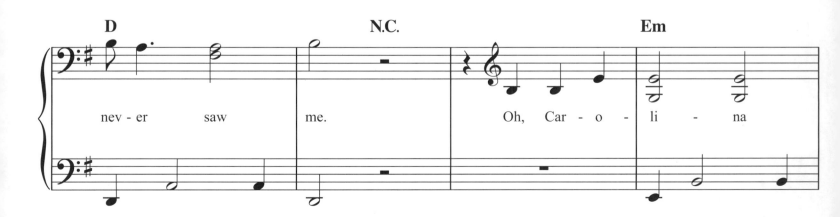

nev - er saw me. Oh, Car - o - li - na

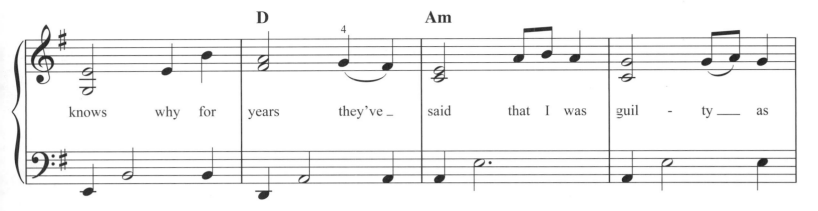

knows why for years they've _ said that I was guil - ty _ as

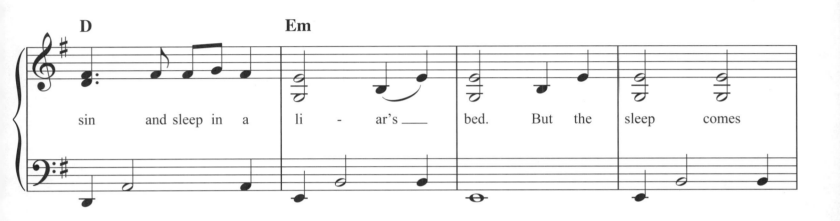

sin and sleep in a li - ar's ___ bed. But the sleep comes

fast and I'll meet no ____ ghosts. It's be - tween

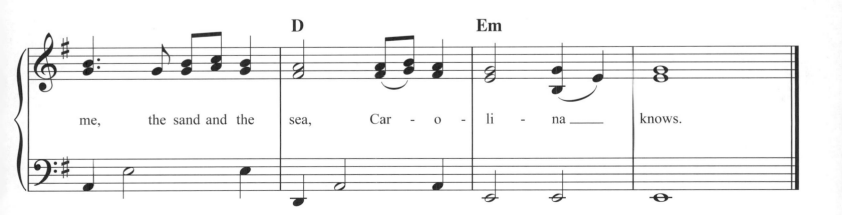

me, the sand and the sea, Car - o - li - na ____ knows.

ENEMY

Words and Music by DANIEL COULTER REYNOLDS,
DANIEL WAYNE SERMON, BENJAMIN ARTHUR McKEE,
DANIEL JAMES PLATZMAN, JUSTIN TRANTER,
MATTIAS LARSSON and ROBIN FREDRIKSSON

back is to the world that was smil - ing when I turned.
show you what it's like to be words spit in a mic.

Tell you you're the great - est, but

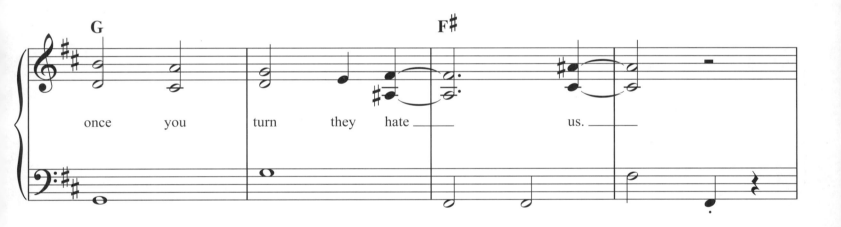

once you turn they hate us.

Oh, the mis - er - y, ev - 'ry - bod - y wants to be my

Rap: (See additional lyrics)

36

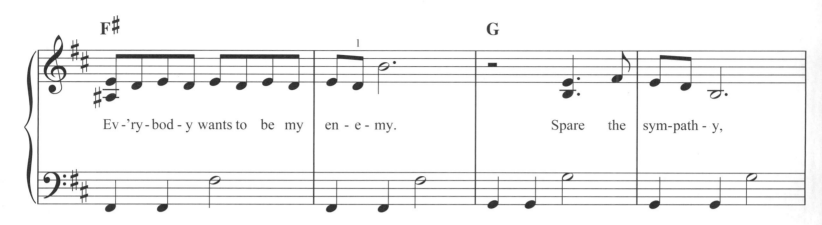

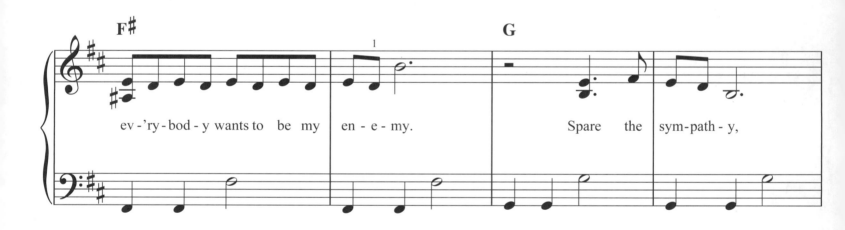

Additional Lyrics

Rap:
Uh, look, okay
I'm hopin' that somebody pray for me
I'm prayin' that somebody hope for me
I'm stayin' where nobody 'posed to be
P-p-posted
Being a wreck of emotions
Ready to go whenever, just let me know
The road is long, so put the pedal into the floor
The enemy on my trail, my energy unavailable
I'm a tell 'em, "Hasta luego"
They wanna plot on my trot to the top
I been outta shape thinkin' out the box, I'm an astronaut
I blasted off the planet rock to cause catastrophe
And it matters more because I had it not
Had I thought about wreaking havoc
On an opposition, kinda shockin' they wanted static
With precision, I'm automatic quarterback
I ain't talkin' sackin', pack it
Pack it up, I don't panic, batter up
Who the baddest? It don't matter 'cause we at you throat

FREEDOM

Words and Music by TIERCE PERSON,
AUTUMN ROWE, ANDRAE ALEXANDER
and JONATHAN BATISTE

Free to live ___ (how I wan-na live), I'm 'on' get

(what I'm gon-na get) 'cause it's my free ___ dom. ___ I love how you talk,

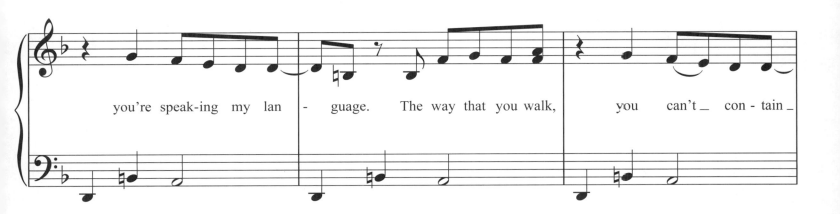

you're speak-ing my lan - guage. The way that you walk, you can't __ con-tain __

___ it. Is it the shoes? ___ Jumped up, kan-ga-roo. ___ We're o - ver - due __

for a lit-tle more pranc - ing. Now is your time,___ (it's your right) you can shine___

___ (it's al - right). ___ If you do, ___ I'm - a do too. ___

When I move my bod - y just like this, I don't know why, but I feel like

free - dom. ___ I hear a song ___ that takes me back, and I

this ain't no drill. More than cheap thrills.

Now is your time, (it's your right) you can shine (it's al - right). If you do,

I'm - a do too. 'Cause when I look up to the

stars I know ex - act - ly who we are, 'cause then I

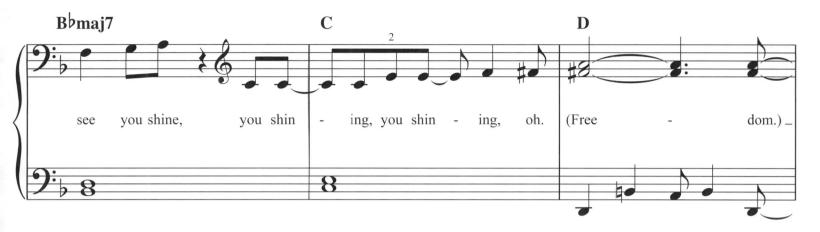

see you shine, you shin - ing, you shin - ing, oh. (Free - dom.)

Come on. I'm stuck to the dance floor with the, with the whole tape, with the,

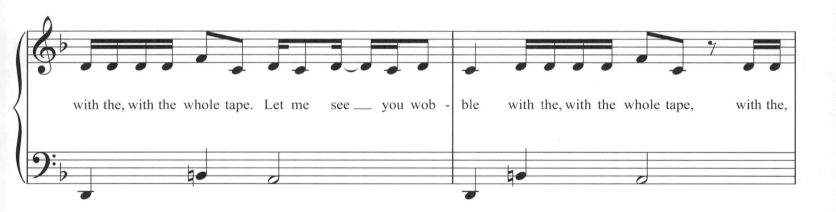

with the, with the whole tape. Let me see you wob - ble with the, with the whole tape, with the,

with the, with the whole tape. Let me see you shake. Giv-ing you the whole shake, I'm - a

give you the whole shake. Let me see __ you wob - ble with the, with the whole tape, with the,

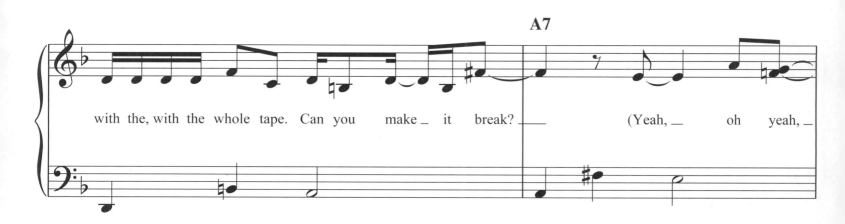

with the, with the whole tape. Can you make __ it break? ___ (Yeah, __ oh yeah, __

___ oh yeah.) Let me see __ you wob - ble.'Cause you do, I'm - a do too.

When I move my bod - y just like this, I don't know why, but I feel like

GLIMPSE OF US

Words and Music by JOJI KUSUNOKI,
CONNOR McDONOUGH, RILEY McDONOUGH,
JOEL CASTILLO and ALEXIS KESSELMAN

Moderately slow, in 2

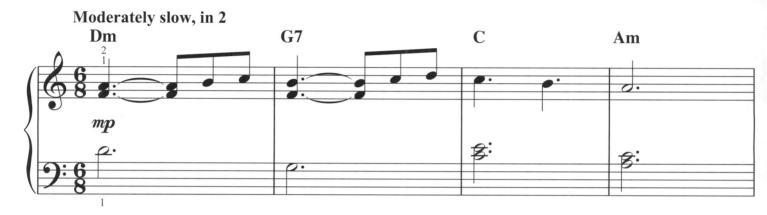

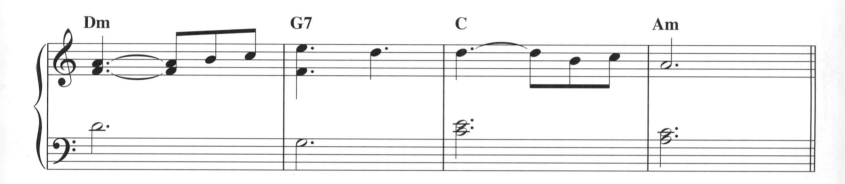

She'd take the world ___ off my shoul - ders, ___ if it was ev - er hard to move. ___
Tell me he sa - vors your glo - ry. ___ Does he laugh the way I did? ___

___ She'd turn the rain ___ to a rain - bow when I was
Is this a part ___ of your sto - ry, one that

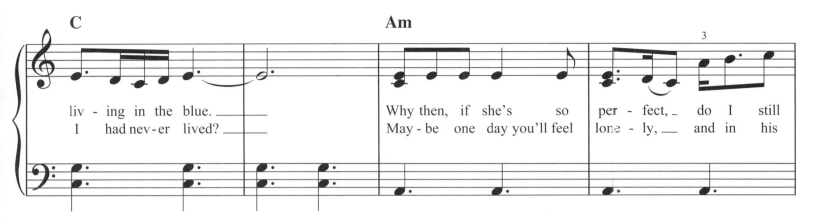

C   Am

liv - ing in the blue. _____
I had nev-er lived? _____

Why then, if she's   so   per - fect, _ do I still
May - be one day you'll feel   lone - ly, _ and in his

Dm7   Dm11   G7

wish   that   it   was you?
eyes   you'll get   a glimpse.

Per - fect don't mean   that it's
May - be you'll start   slip - ping

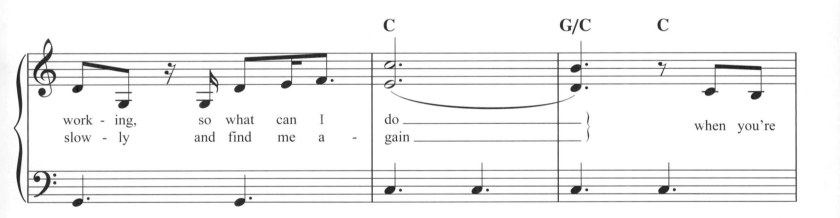

                         C   G/C   C

work - ing,   so what can I
slow - ly   and find me a -

do _____
gain _____

when you're

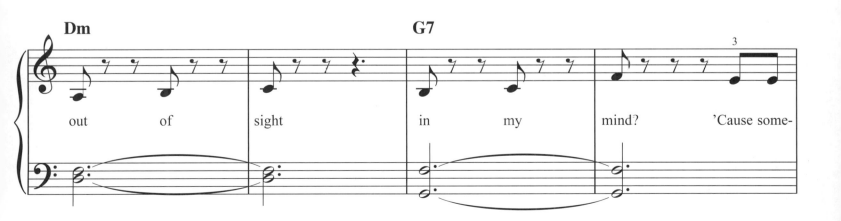

Dm   G7

out   of   sight   in   my   mind?   'Cause some-

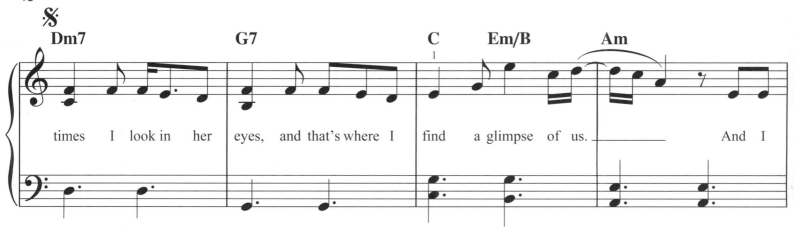

times I look in her eyes, and that's where I find a glimpse of us. _____ And I

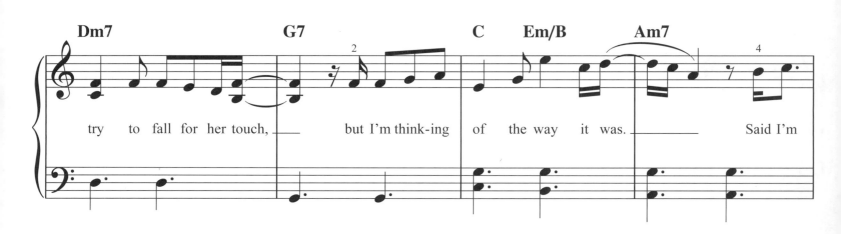

try to fall for her touch, ____ but I'm think-ing of the way it was. _____ Said I'm

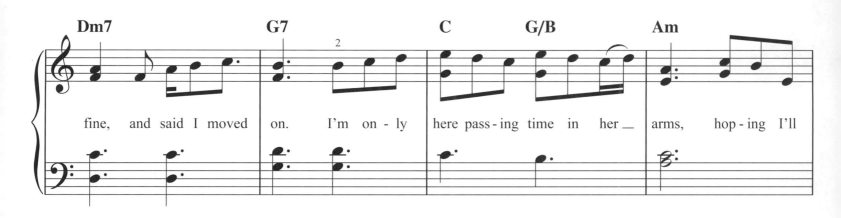

fine, and said I moved on. I'm on-ly here pass-ing time in her __ arms, hop-ing I'll

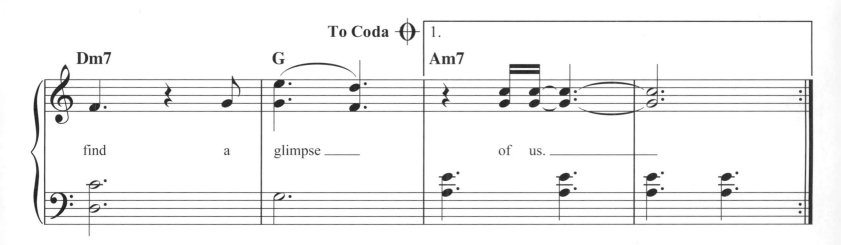

find a glimpse _____ of us. _____

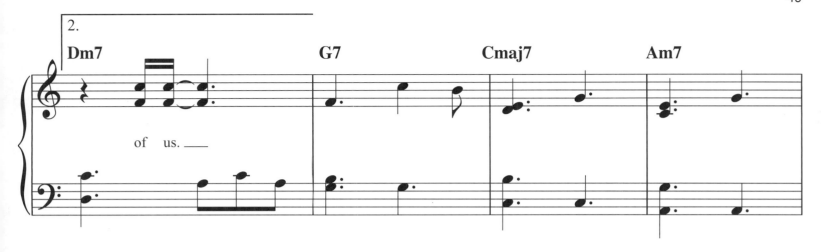

of us. ___

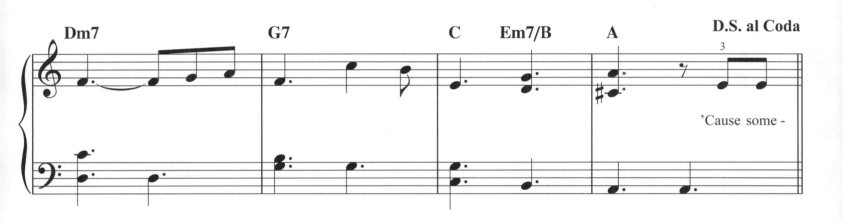

'Cause some -

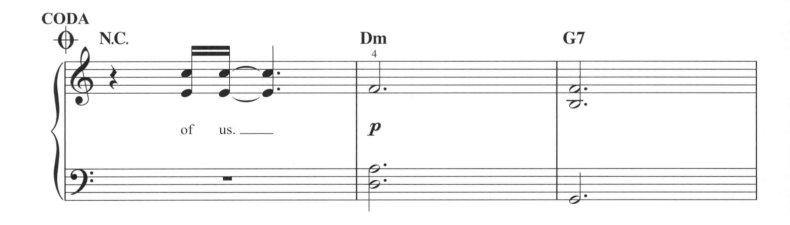

of us. ___

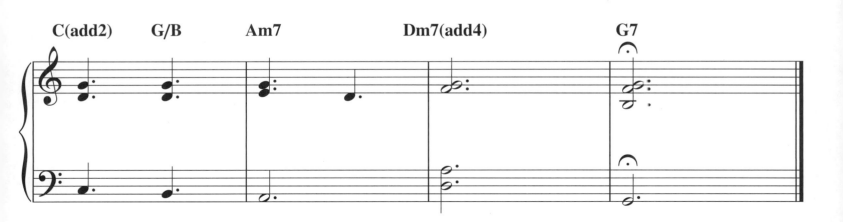

HOLD MY HAND
from TOP GUN: MAVERICK

Words and Music by STEFANI GERMANOTTA
and MICHAEL TUCKER

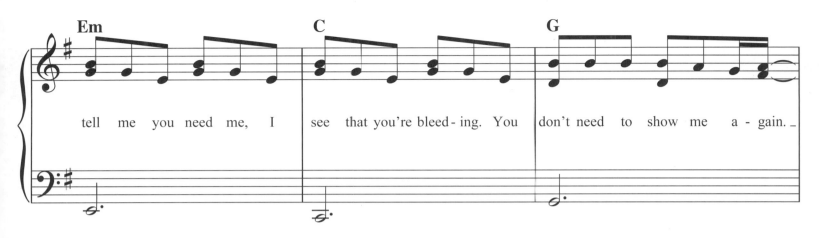

tell me you need me, I see that you're bleed-ing. You don't need to show me a-gain. __

__ But if you de-cide to, I'll ride in this life with you,

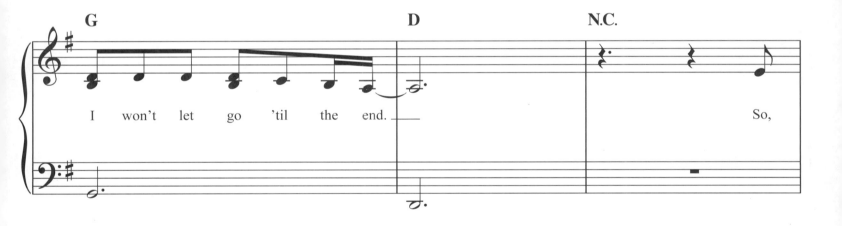

I won't let go 'til the end. __ So,

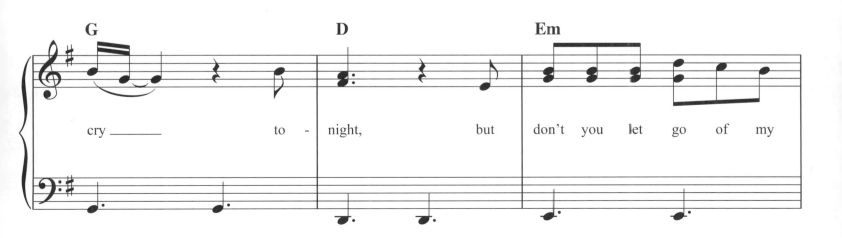

cry __ to - night, but don't you let go of my

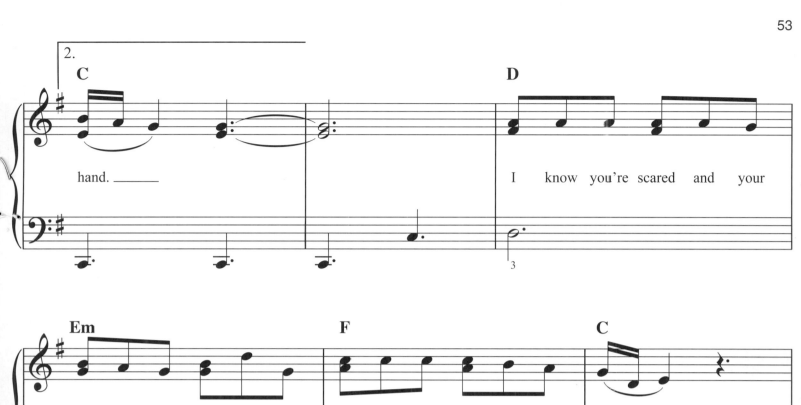

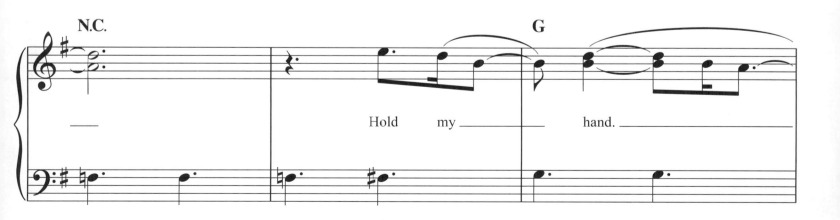

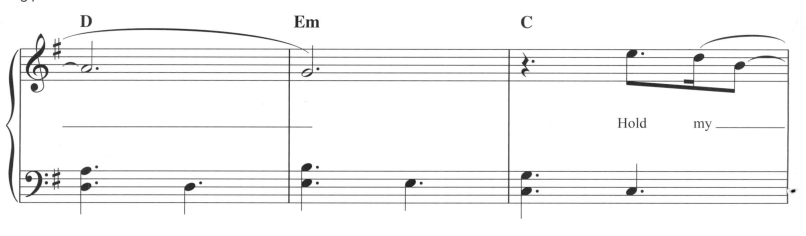

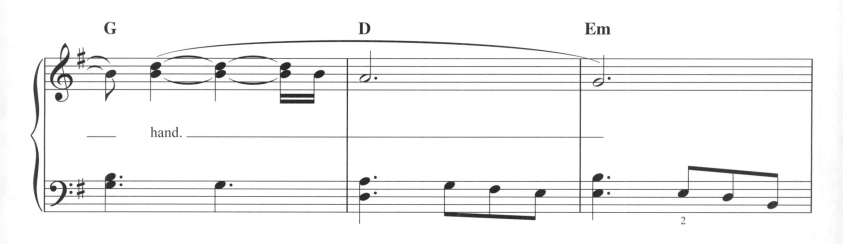

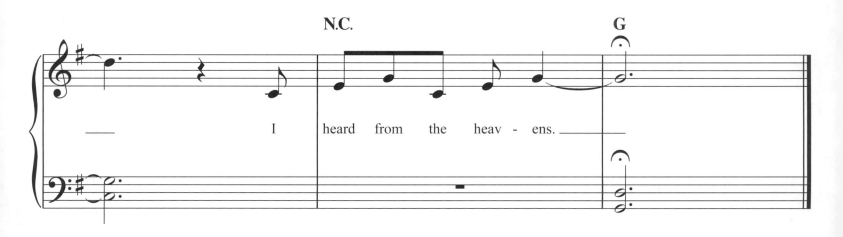

LOVE ME MORE

Words and Music by SAM SMITH,
TOR HERMANSEN, JAMES NAPIER
and MIKKEL ERIKSEN

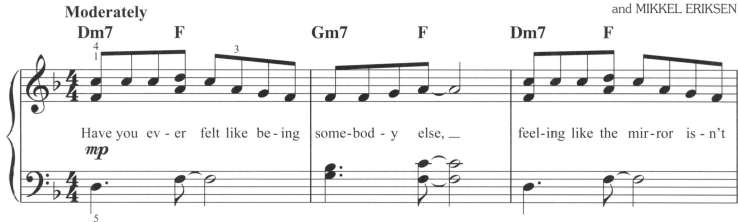

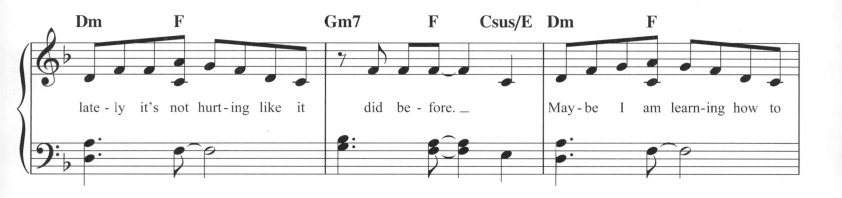

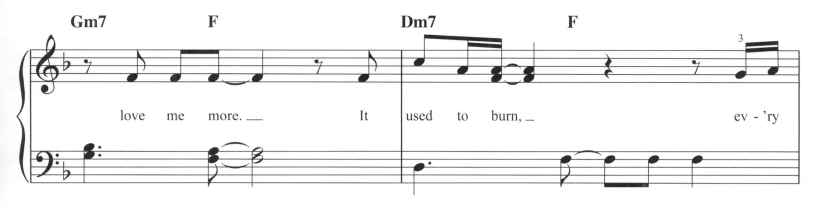

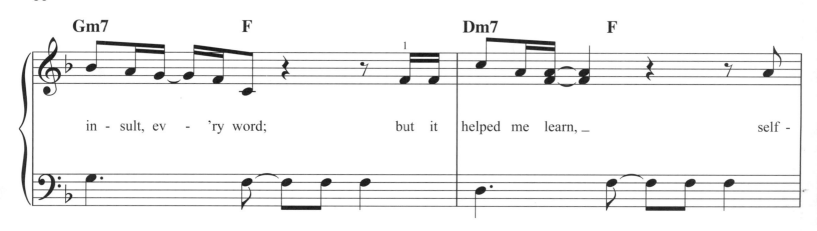

in - sult, ev - 'ry word; but it helped me learn, __ self-

worth I had __ to earn. So I tried ev - 'ry night to

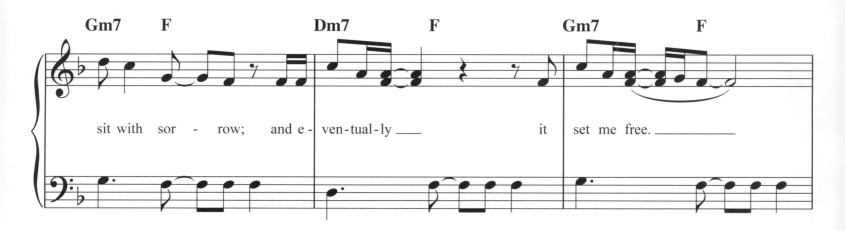

sit with sor - row; and e - ven-tual-ly __ it set me free. __

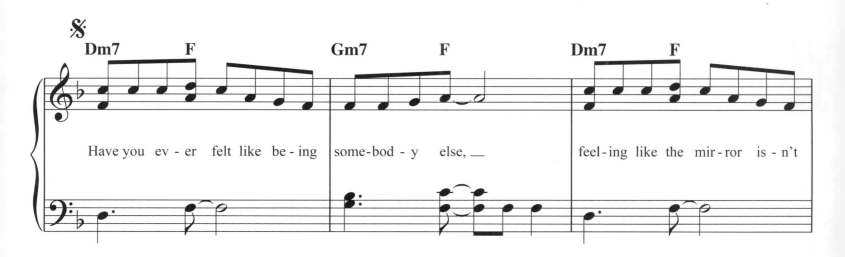

Have you ev - er felt like be - ing some-bod - y else, __ feel-ing like the mir - ror is - n't

good for your health? _   Ev -'ry day I'm try - ing not to   hate my - self, ___   but

late - ly it's not hurt - ing like it   did be - fore. _   May - be I am learn-ing how to

love me more,   just a lit-tle bit.   Love me more,   just a lit-tle bit.   Love me more,   oh, no. ___

To Coda

Love me more,   just a lit - tle bit.   Love me more.   I   used to cry _____   my-

self to sleep __ at night. I'd blame the sky _____ when the

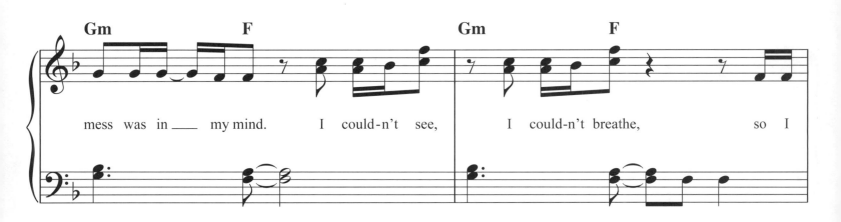

mess was in __ my mind. I could-n't see, I could-n't breathe, so I

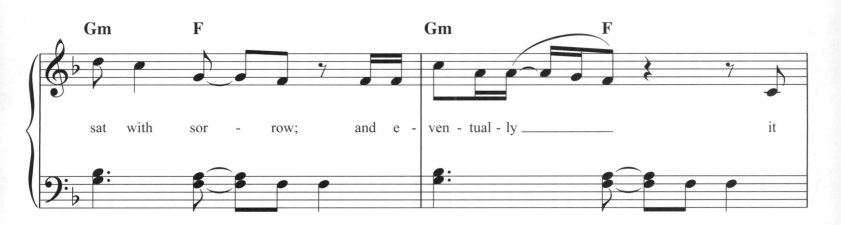

sat with sor - row; and e - ven-tual-ly _____ it

set me free. _____

Love me more. Yeah.

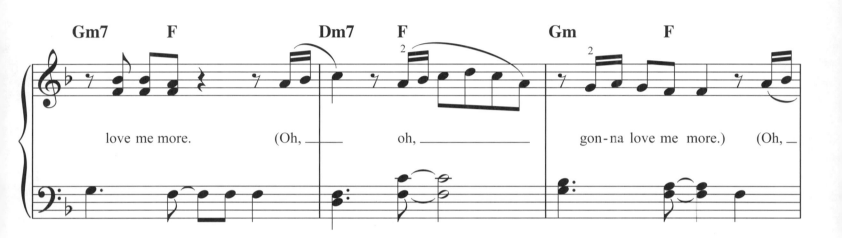

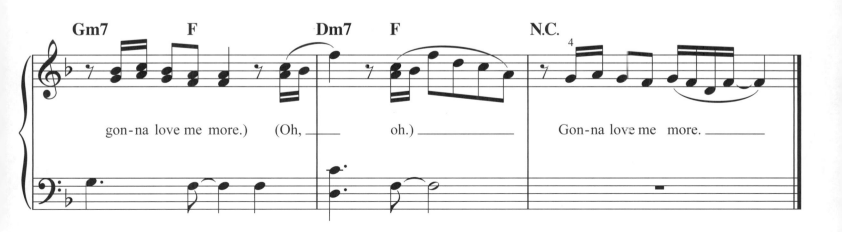

LIGHT SWITCH

Words and Music by CHARLIE PUTH,
JACOB KASHER HINDLIN and JACOB TORREY

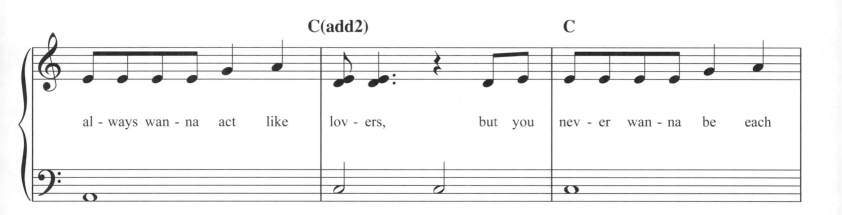

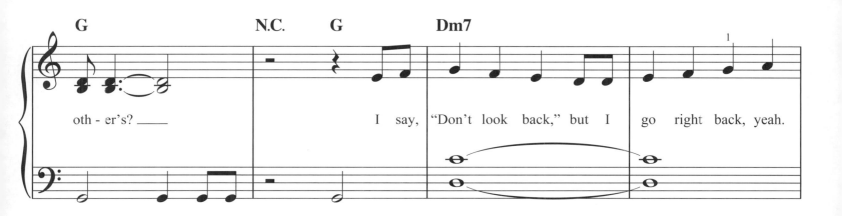

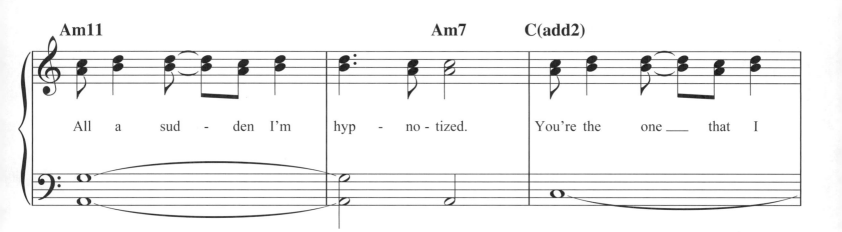

can't de - ny. Ev -'ry time __ that I say I'm gon - na walk a -

way... You turn me on like a light switch when you're mov - ing your bod -

- y a - round __ and a - round. _____ Now I ___ don't wan - na fight this.

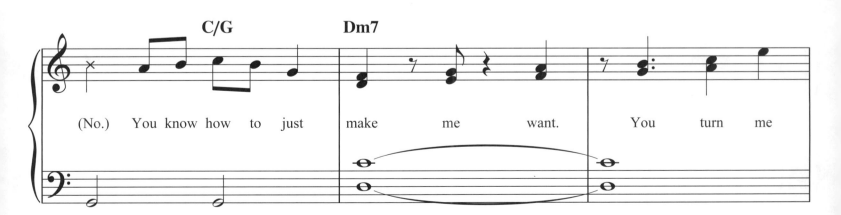

(No.) You know how to just make me want. You turn me

on like a light switch when you're mov-ing your bod - y a - round _ and a - round. _

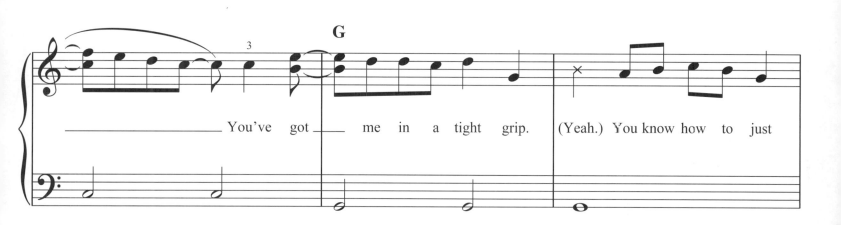

_____ You've got _ me in a tight grip. (Yeah.) You know how to just

make me want you, ba - by. you, ba - by. _____ Come on, _

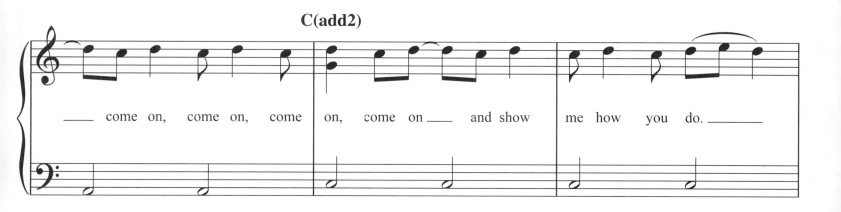

_ come on, come on, come on, come on _ and show me how you do. _

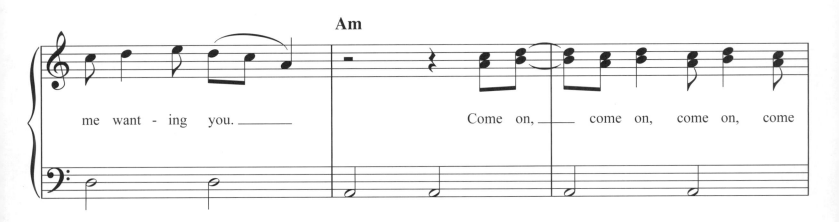

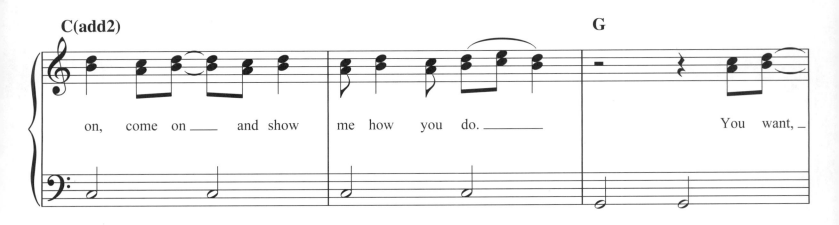

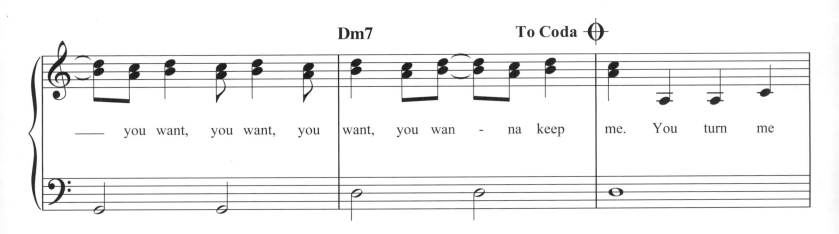

on like a light switch   when you're mov-ing your bod - y a-round __ and a-round. __

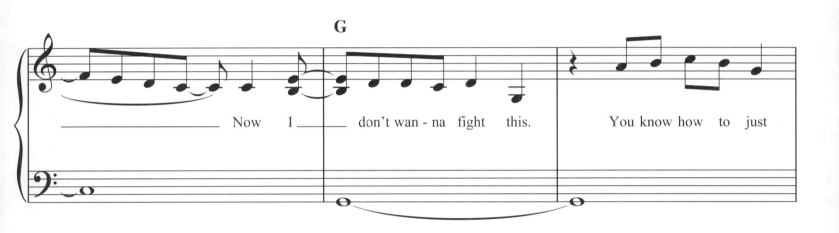

_____ Now I ___ don't wan-na fight this.   You know how to just

D.S. al Coda
(take 3rd ending)

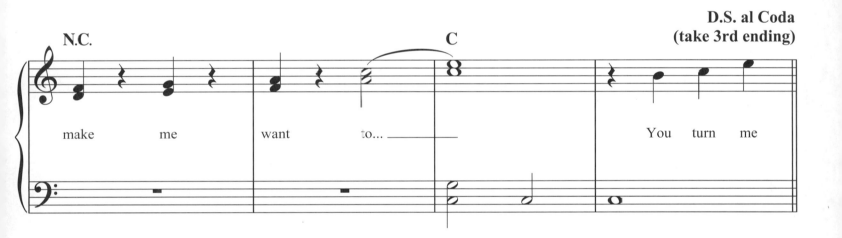

make   me   want   to... ___ ___   You turn me

me want-ing you. ___   (Click.)

NOBODY LIKE U
from TURNING RED

Music and Lyrics by BILLIE EILISH
and FINNEAS O'CONNELL

Moderate groove

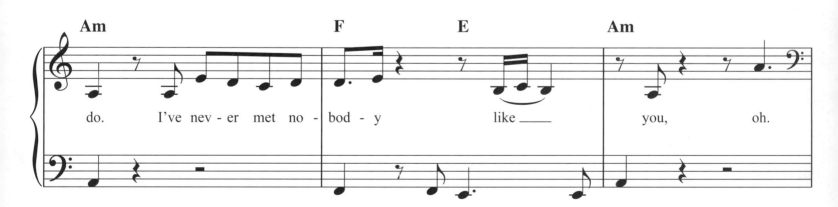

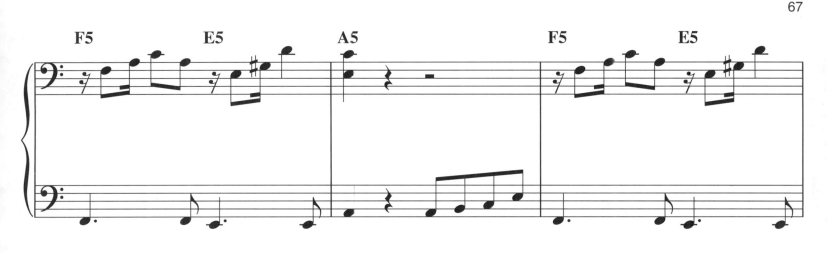

Youre nev-er not on my mind, oh my, oh my. I'm nev-er not by your

side, your side, your side. I'm nev-er gon-na let you cry, oh cry, don't

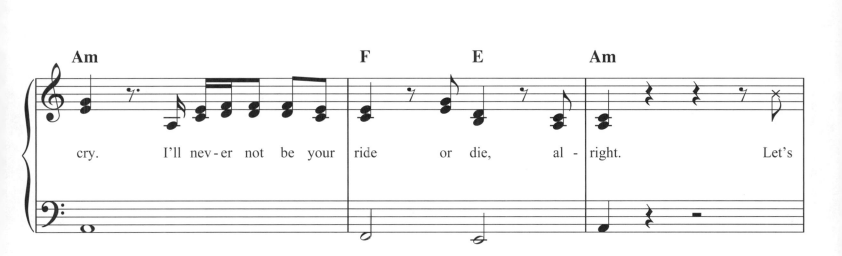

cry. I'll nev-er not be your ride or die, al - right. Let's

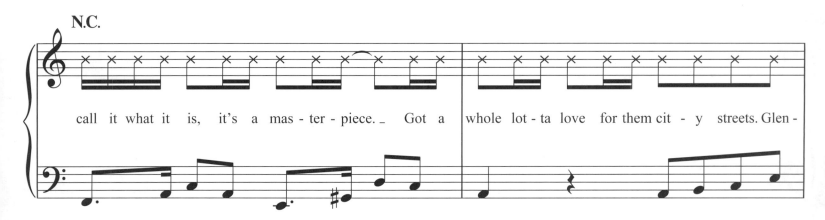

N.C.

call it what it is, it's a mas-ter-piece. __ Got a whole lot-ta love for them cit - y streets. Glen-

dale to-night, is the place to be __ got a big boom box and a new C - D. __ Come on __

__ ev -'ry-bod -y let's tear it up. __ If you want mad skills, you can share with us. __ I want __

__ ev -'ry-bod -y to stop and stare __ and you know why, it's me Ro - baire.

N.C.

Li, li, li, li, li, like you. Li, li, li, li, li, like you.

1.

Li, li, li, li, li, like you. Like _ you, like _ you.

2.

Li, li, li, li, li, like you.

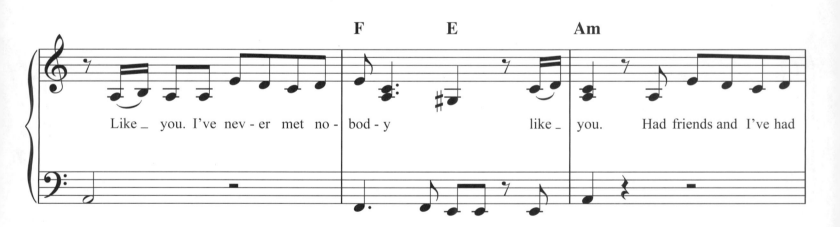

F   E   Am

Like _ you. I've nev - er met no - bod - y   like _ you.   Had friends and I've had

F   E   Am   F   E

bud - dies   it's _ true.   But they don't turn my   tum - my   the way _ you

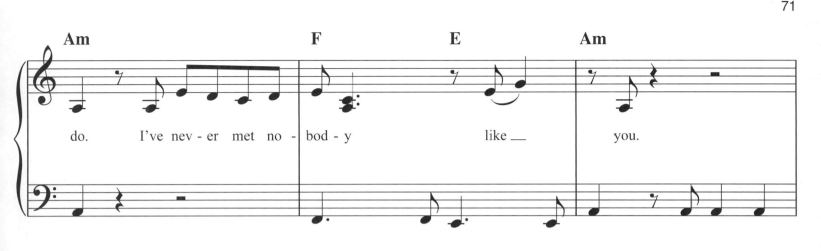

NUMB LITTLE BUG

Words and Music by EMILY BEIHOLD,
NICHOLAS LOPEZ and ANDREW DeCARO

caught up with my friends in weeks __ and now __ we're out - ta touch. I've been

driv - in' in L. A. __ and the world, it feels __ too big. __ Like a

float - ing ball that's bound to break, __ snap my psy - che like a twig. And I

Fmaj7   **Fm7**

just wan - na see __ if you feel the same as __ me. Do you ev - er get a

lit-tle bit tired of life? Like you're not — real-ly hap-py but you don't wan-na die? Like you're hang-in' by a

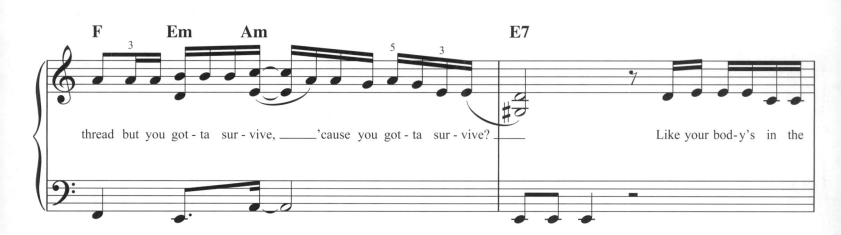

thread but you got-ta sur-vive, _____ 'cause you got-ta sur-vive? _____ Like your bod-y's in the

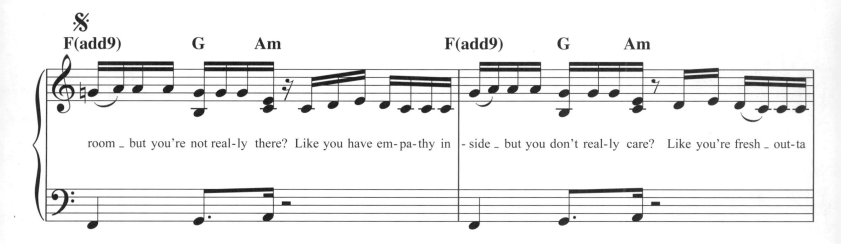

room _ but you're not real-ly there? Like you have em-pa-thy in - side _ but you don't real-ly care? Like you're fresh _ out-ta

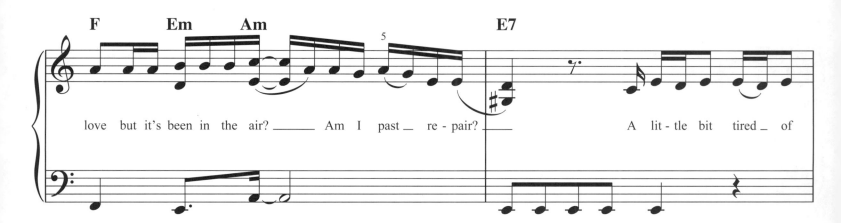

love but it's been in the air? _____ Am I past _ re-pair? _____ A lit-tle bit tired _ of

F   C   G

tryin'   to   care   when   I   don't.   A   lit - tle   but   tired ___ of

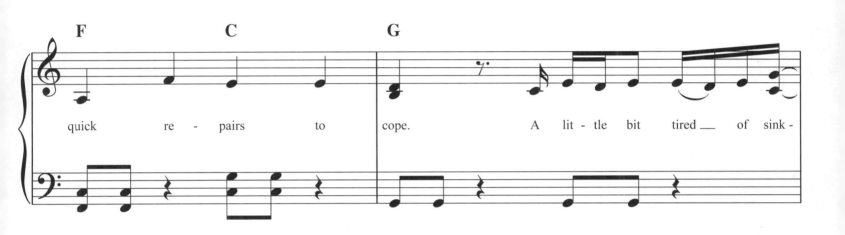

F   C   G

quick   re - pairs   to   cope.   A   lit - tle   bit   tired ___ of   sink-

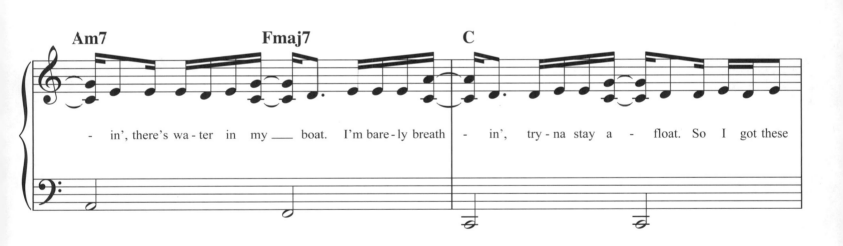

Am7   Fmaj7   C

- in', there's wa - ter   in   my ___ boat.   I'm bare - ly breath - in',   try - na stay a - float. So   I   got these

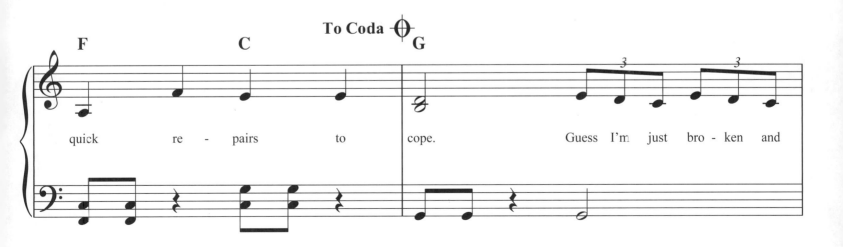

To Coda ⊕

F   C   G

quick   re - pairs   to   cope.   Guess   I'm   just   bro - ken   and

broke.   The pre- scrip-tions's on its way ___   with a

name   I can't pro - nounce. _   And the   dose   I   got - ta   take, __   boy, I

Fmaj7

wish   that   I   could count.   'Cause I   just   wan - na   see ___   if ___ this   could

Fm7   **N.C.**

make me   hap - py.   Do you ev - er get a   lit - tle bit   tired of life?   Like you're not __ real - ly

hap-py but you don't wan-na die? Like you're hang-in' by a thread but you got-ta sur-vive, _____ 'cause you got-ta sur-vive? _

D.S. al Coda

CODA

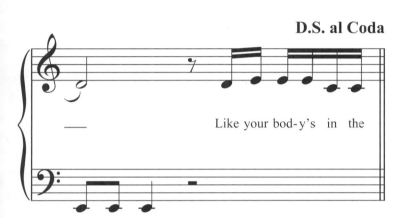

_____ Like your bod-y's in the

G

cope. Do you ev- er get a

Fmaj7 **Em**

lit - tle bit tired of life? _ Like you're not _ real-ly hap-py but you don't wan-na die? _ Like a numb _ lit-tle

Am **C** **D**

bug _ that's got - ta sur - vive, _ that's got - ta sur - vive?

ON MY WAY

from MARRY ME

Words and Music by JAMES CLAMPITT,
IVY ADARA and MICHAEL POLLACK

Slow Ballad

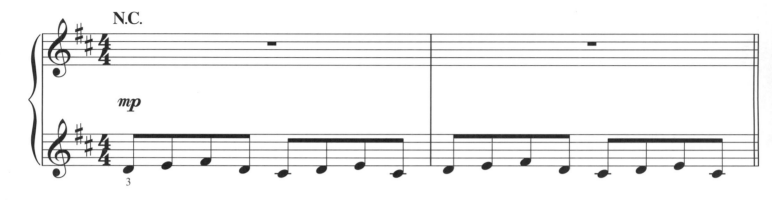

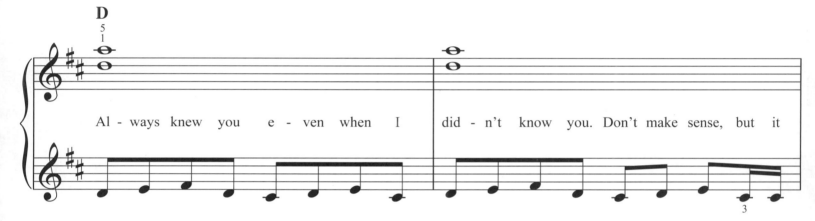

Al - ways knew you e - ven when I did - n't know you. Don't make sense, but it

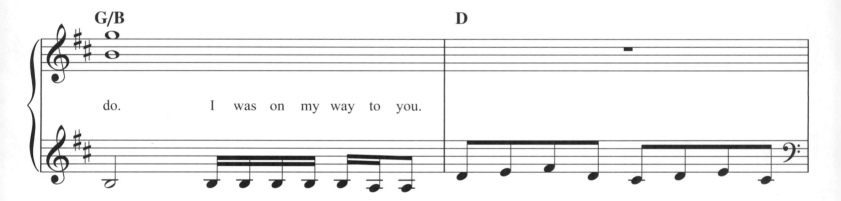

do.   I was on my way to you.

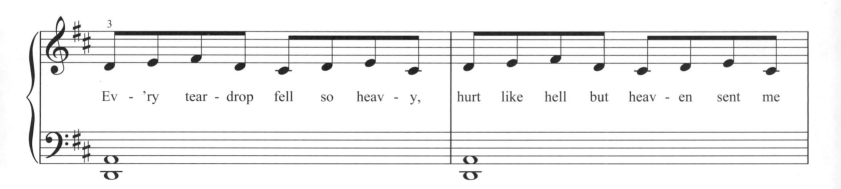

Ev - 'ry tear - drop fell so heav - y, hurt like hell but heav - en sent me

G / **D**

through. I was on my way to you. And

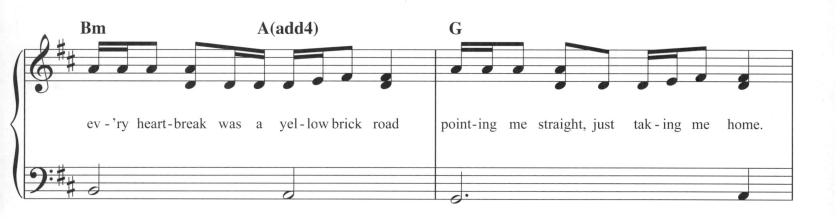

Bm / **A(add4)** / **G**

ev-'ry heart-break was a yel-low brick road point-ing me straight, just tak-ing me home.

Bm / **A(add4)** / **G**

I was nev-er lost,_____ I was just pass-ing through. I was on my way to you.__

D

_____ Hope was hope-less, faith was run-ning.

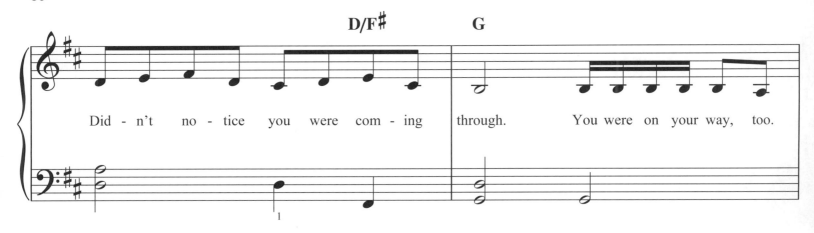

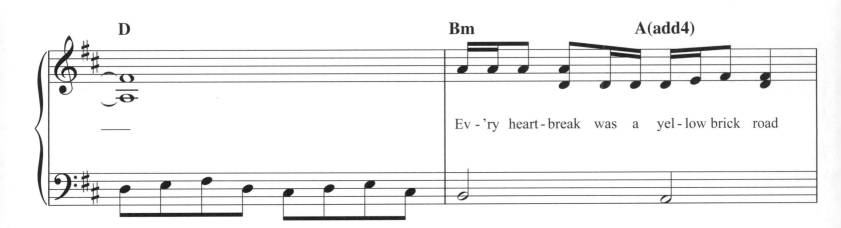

G   **Bm**   **A(add4)**

point-ing me straight, just tak-ing me home.   I was nev-er lost, _____ I was just pass-ing

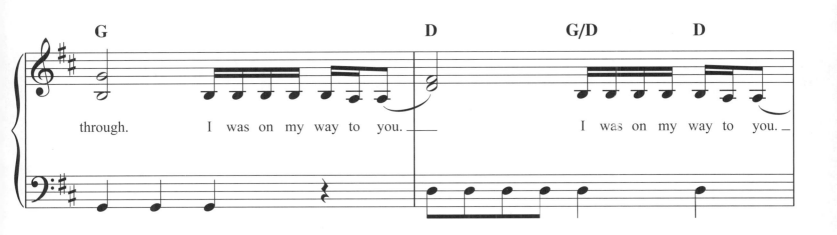

G   **D**   **G/D**   **D**

through.   I was on my way to you. _____   I was on my way to you. _____

G   **Bm**

_____   I was on my way to you. _____   I was on my way to you. _____

A   **D**   **D/F♯**

_____   Oh, _____ I'm on _____ my way, on _____ my way to you. On _____

___ my way, on ___ my way to you. On ___ my way, on ___ my way to you. ____

___ Oh, _____ I'm on ___ my way, I'm on ___ my way. (On ___

___ my way.) On ___ my way, ___ (On ___ my way.) on ___ my way to you. ____

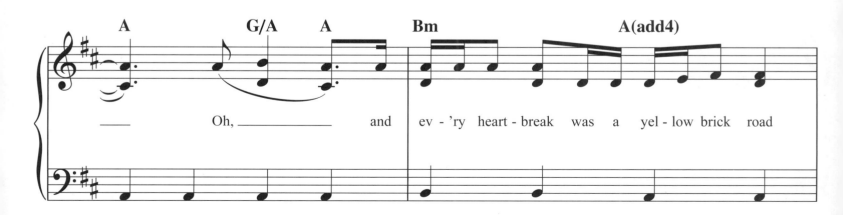

___ Oh, _____ and ev - 'ry heart - break was a yel - low brick road_

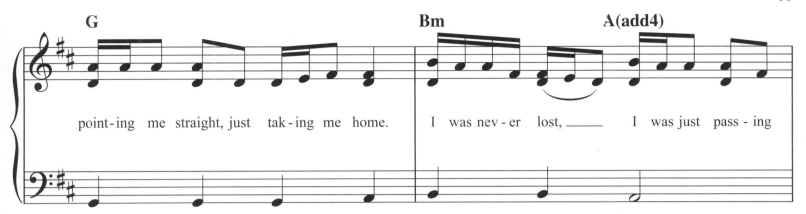

RUNNING UP THAT HILL

featured in the fourth season of the Netflix series STRANGER THINGS

Words and Music by
KATE BUSH

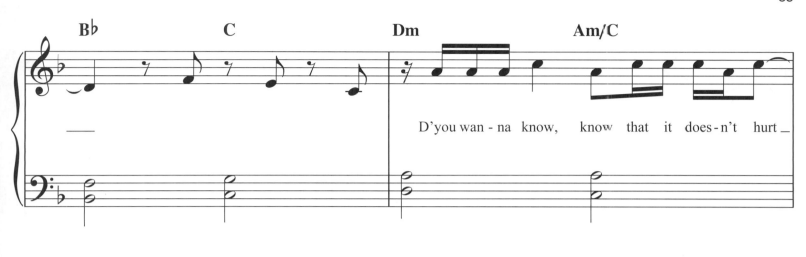

Bb   C   Dm   Am/C

___ D'you wan - na know, know that it does-n't hurt ___

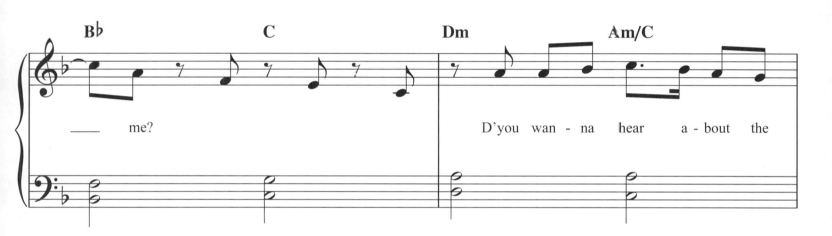

Bb   C   Dm   Am/C

___ me?   D'you wan - na hear a - bout the

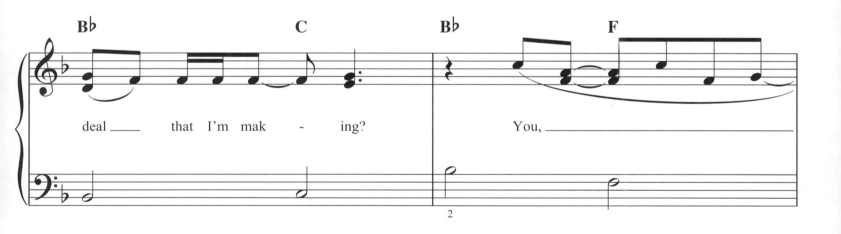

Bb   C   Bb   F

deal ___ that I'm mak - ing?   You, _____

Gm   Bb   F   Gm

___   it's you and me. _____   And

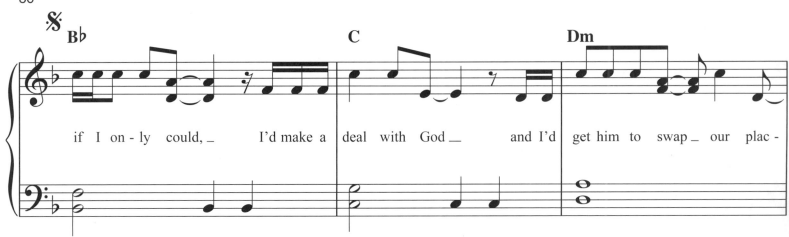

if I on-ly could, __ I'd make a deal with God __ and I'd get him to swap __ our plac-

- es. Be run-ning up that road, ____ be run-ning up that hill, ____ be run-ning up that build-

- ing. ____ See if I on-ly could, ____

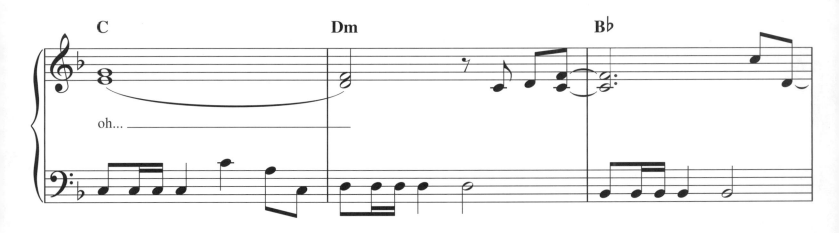

oh... ____

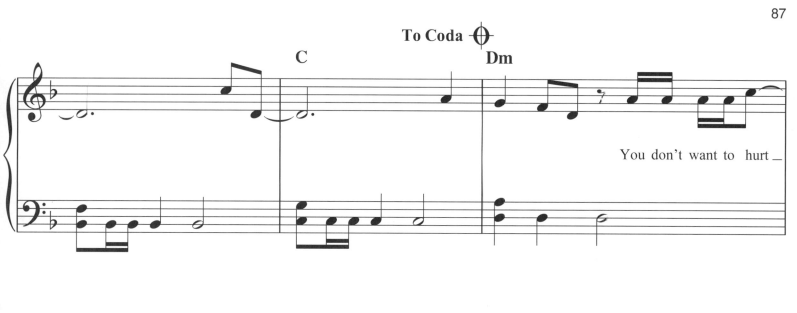

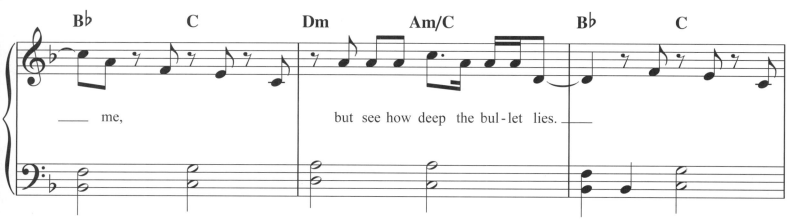

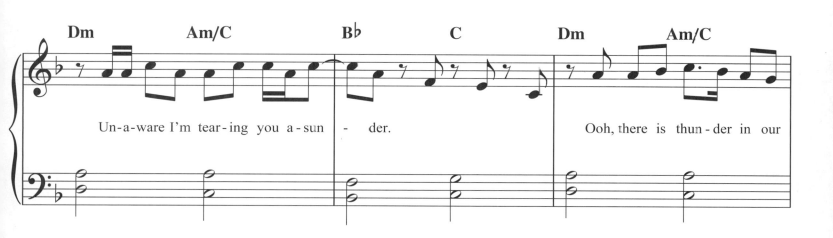

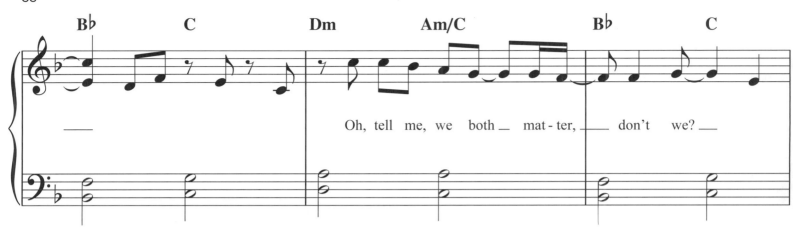

Oh, tell me, we both __ mat - ter, __ don't we? __

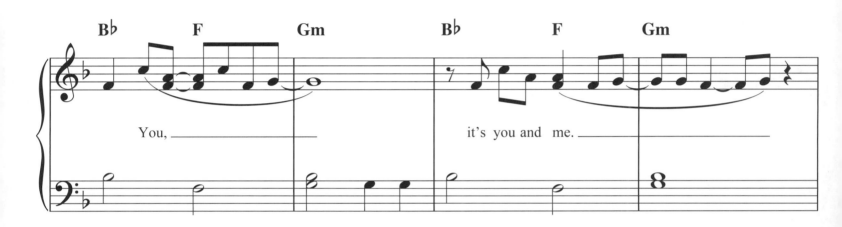

You, _____ it's you and me. _____

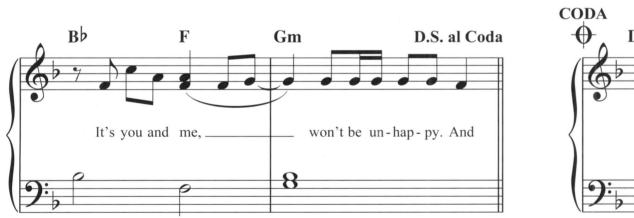

It's you and me, _____ won't be un - hap - py. And

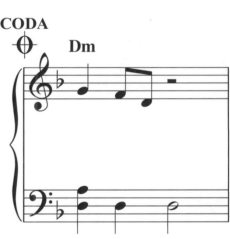

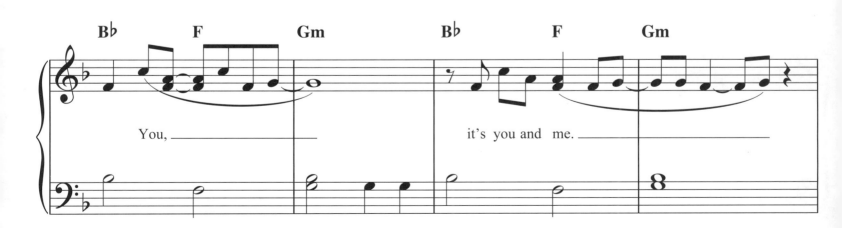

You, _____ it's you and me. _____

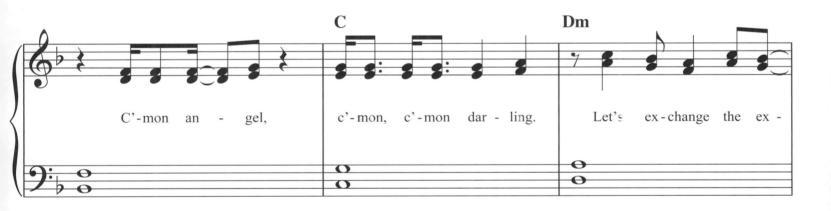

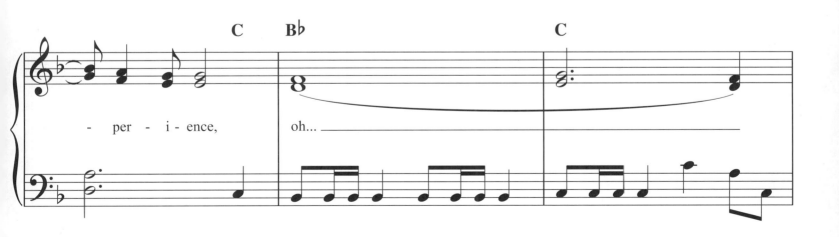

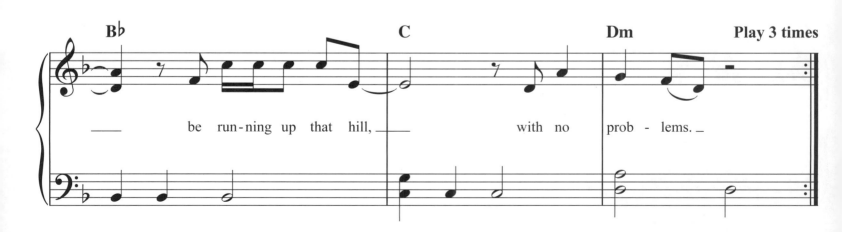

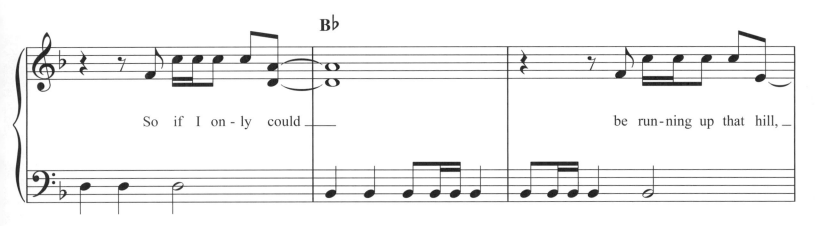

So if I on-ly could ___ be run-ning up that hill, ___

___ with no prob-lems. ___

If I on - ly could, ___ I'd be run-ning up that hill.

If I on - ly could, ___ I'd be run-ning up that hill. ___

'TIL YOU CAN'T

Words and Music by BEN STENNIS
and MATT ROGERS

Country Rock

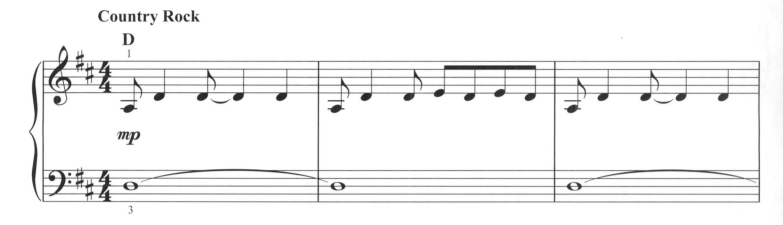

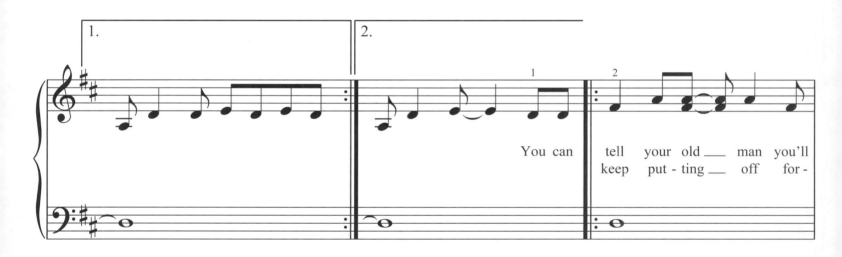

1.
do some large - mouth

2.
You can tell your old ___ man you'll
keep put - ting ___ off for -

do some large - mouth fish - ing an - oth - er time. ___ You just ___
ev - er with ___ that girl who's heart you hold. ___ Swear-

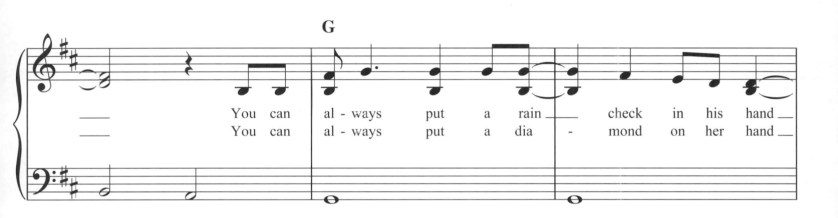

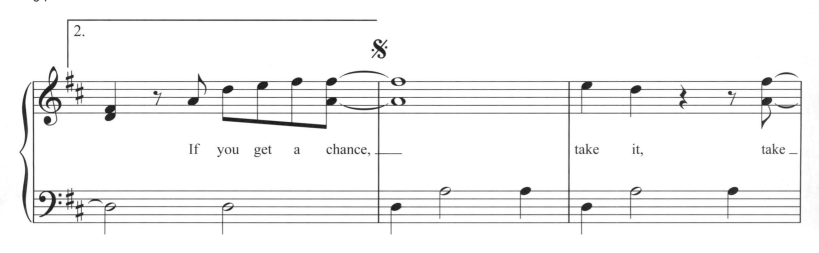

If you get a chance, _____ take it, take _

_ it while you've got a chance. ____ If you've got a dream, ____

chase it 'cause a dream ___ won't chase you back. ____ If you're gon - na love _

___ some - bod - y, hold them as long _ and as strong __ and as close _ as you can _

'til you can't.

There's a box of greas - y parts ___ sit - ting in the trunk ___

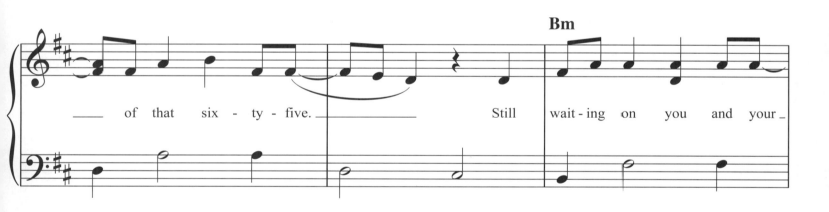

___ of that six - ty - five. ___ Still wait - ing on you and your ___

___ grand - dad to bring it back ___ to life. ___ You can

al-ways get a-round to fix-ing up that Pon-ti-ac 'til you can't.

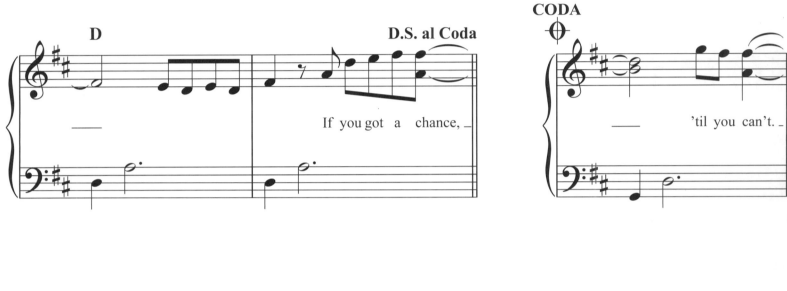

D.S. al Coda

CODA

If you got a chance, 'til you can't.

So take that

phone call from your ma - ma and just talk a-way.

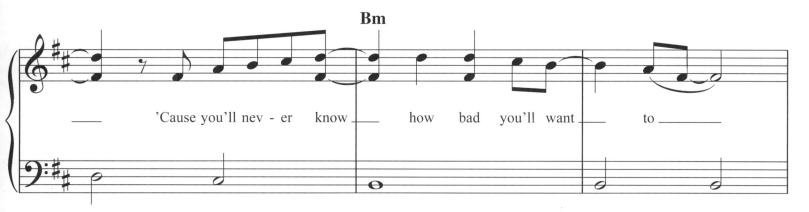

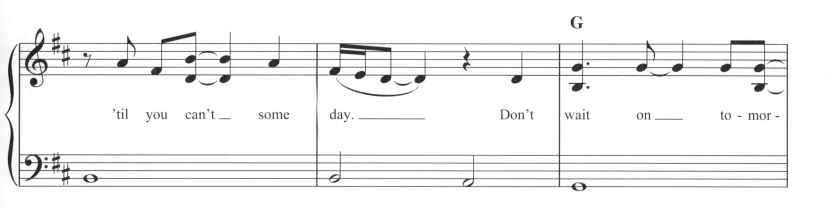

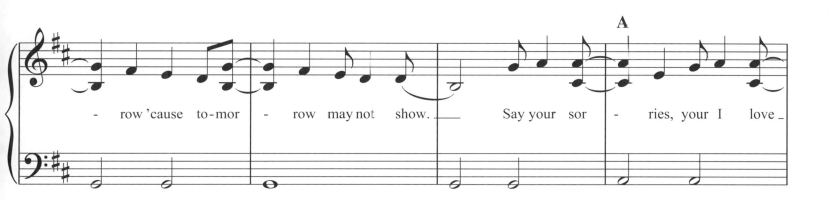

take it, take it while you've got a chance.

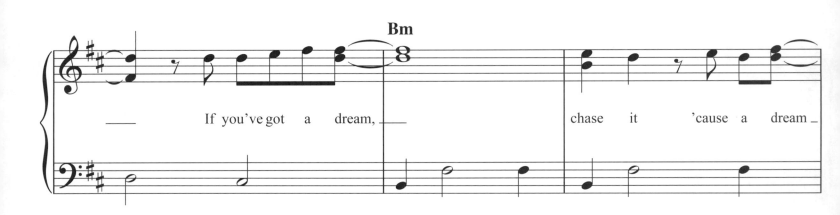

If you've got a dream, chase it 'cause a dream

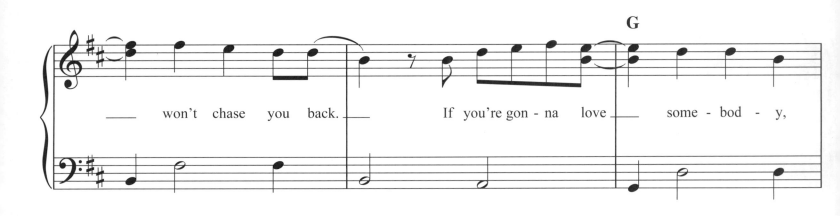

won't chase you back. If you're gon-na love some-bod-y,

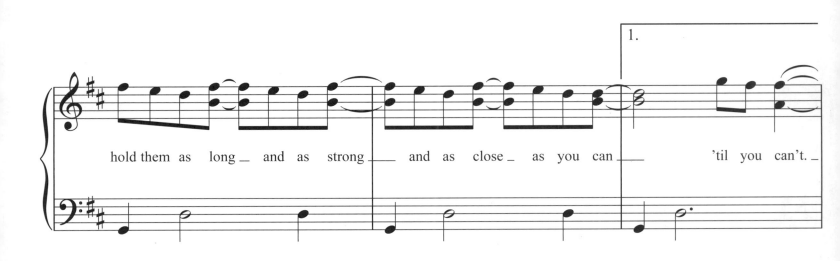

hold them as long and as strong and as close as you can 'til you can't.

UNTIL I FOUND YOU

Words and Music by EMILY BEIHOLD
and STEPHEN SANCHEZ

Moderate Ballad

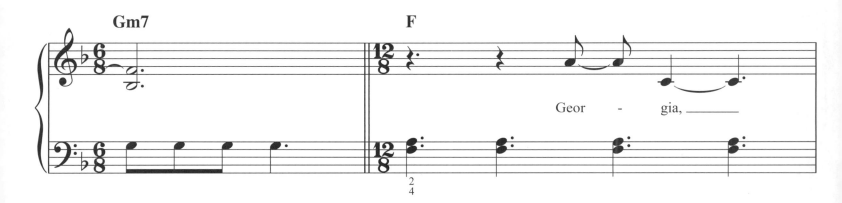

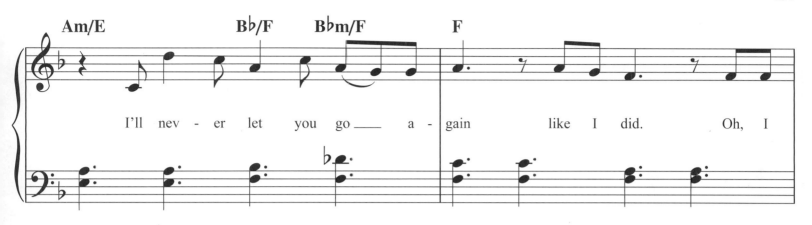

I'll nev-er let you go___ a-gain like I did. Oh, I

used to___ say I would nev-er fall in love a-gain un-til

I found___ her. I said I would nev-er fall un-less it's

you I fall___ in-to.___ I was lost with-in the dark-ness, but then

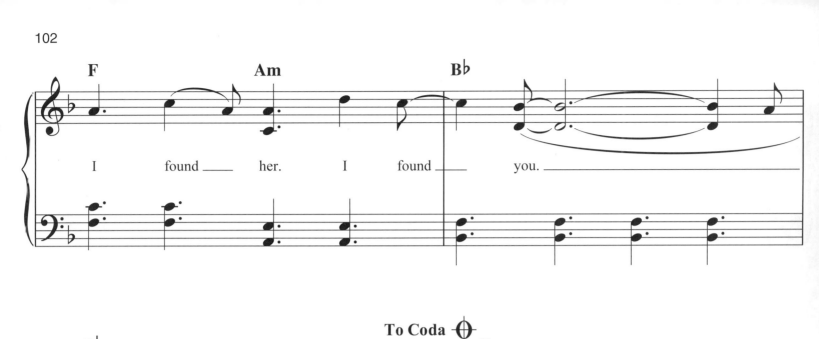

I found ____ her. I found ____ you. ____

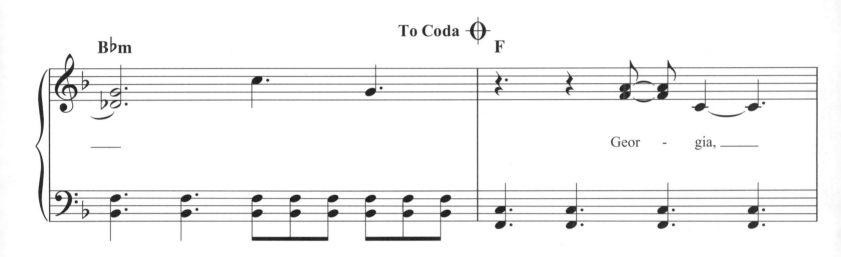

To Coda

____ Geor - gia, ____

pulled me in, I asked to ____ love her. ____

Once a - gain, you fell, I ____ caught you. ____

I'll nev - er let you go _____ a - gain   like I did.   Oh, I

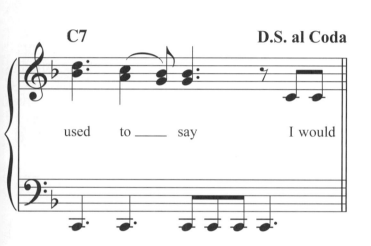

used   to _____ say   I would

I would nev - er fall   in love   a - gain un - til

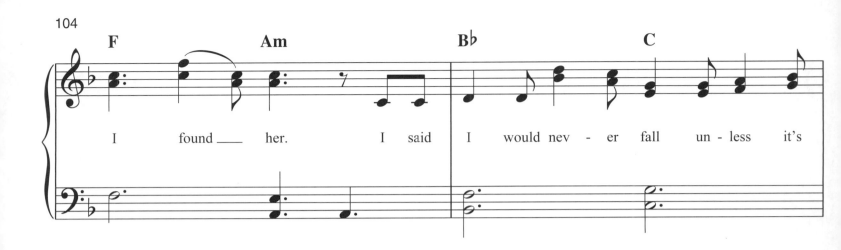

I found ___ her. I said I would nev - er fall un - less it's

you I fall ___ in - to. ___ I was lost with - in the dark - ness, but then

I found ___ her. I found ___ you. ___

___ *rit.*